John Richardson is an autho hospitality industry where he s owners increase profits and m efficiently. He has worked wit ᵍ⌐ᵉ ᵒⁱᵗᵉ operators to chains with multiple sites and turnover in the hundreds of millions. Before becoming an advisor to the industry, John built and sold a wide range of hospitality businesses on his own behalf – including sandwich bars, coffee shops, restaurants, bars and garden centres. His first job, at the age of fourteen, was cleaning tables at Morelli's famous ice cream café in Portstewart.

Currently running a number of businesses, **Hugh Gilmartin** leads a team of coffee experts in the pursuit of sensual experiences in the business of coffee. He is dedicated to growing other people's businesses, and in doing so, his own, through the use of proven models, tools and processes. With a massive focus on measurement, data validation decision-making, clarity of purpose and straight-talking, he helps build the capability of the business owners and managers he works with. He is based in Northern Ireland but works extensively outside it. He can be reached at www.specialistbeverages.com.

Also by John Richardson and Hugh Gilmartin

Wake Up and Smell The Profit – 52 Guaranteed Ways
To Make More Money In Your Coffee Business

The Coffee Boys' Step-by-step Guide To
Setting Up and Managing A Coffee Bar

Wake Up and Sell More Coffee

John Richardson
Hugh Gilmartin

A HOW TO BOOK

ROBINSON

ROBINSON

First published in Great Britain in 2015 by Robinson

Copyright © John Richardson, 2015
1 3 5 7 9 8 6 4 2

A CIP catalogue record for this book
is available from the British Library.

ISBN 978-1-47213-596-4 (paperback)

Typeset by TW Typesetting, Plymouth, Devon
Printed and bound in Great Britain by CPI Group (UK) Ltd,
Croydon CR0 4YY
Papers used by Robinson are from well-managed forests and other responsible sources

MIX
Paper from
responsible sources
FSC® C104740

Robinson
is an imprint of
Little, Brown Book Group
Carmelite House
50 Victoria Embankment
London EC4Y 0DZ

An Hachette UK Company
www.hachette.co.uk

www.littlebrown.co.uk

How To Books are published by Robinson, an imprint of Little, Brown Book
Group. We welcome proposals from authors who have first-hand experience
of their subjects. Please set out the aims of your book, its target market and
its suggested contents in an email to Nikki.Read@howtobooks.co.uk

ACKNOWLEDGEMENTS

Johnny
A book like this cannot be produced without a lot of help from others. Huge thanks must go to Helen Marriot and the great team at Caffè Culture for assisting with and giving us the platform to produce the wider research.

Beyond that, we'd like to thank all those who took the time to reply to the surveys and especially those who gave us much longer answers that didn't make the final cut for the book.

Hugo
There are many people that should be thanked in the production of a project like this and the biggest thanks has to go to Johnny, who has tirelessly pulled together so much of this great material. But it is a really important thing to surround yourself with advisors and mentors that will tell you the truth, keep you on track, expertly advise using their unique ability, and also encourage and motivate.

My thanks in no particular order to James Healy, Alan Reid, Patrick Jordan, Se Gorman, Conal Casey, Molly Gilmartin and, crucially, business partner and brother James.

CONTENTS

CONTENTS

PREFACE – ADDITIONAL MATERIAL

As with all our books we wanted to make sure you got a lot more value than that which exists simply on the written page. To that end we have created a special website which holds a wealth of supporting material.

www.wakeupandsellbook.com

Make sure you sign up to receive:

- The full details of the much larger research that we jointly produced with Caffè Culture
- The full presentation we presented at Caffè Culture summarising this research
- Longer, much more in-depth interviews with many of the owners featured in this book
- The webinar showing how we altered our coaching and consulting processes as a result of this book
- Access to the full process we use to help clients focus on getting their exit strategy right.

INTRODUCTION

This book is the third book in a series that Hugh and I have written about coffee shops. Our first book – *Wake Up and Smell the Profit: 52 guaranteed ways to make more money in your coffee business* – was essentially a distillation of the various tips, techniques and ideas that had worked for us in our own businesses over the previous fifteen to twenty years. But there was little or no structure to these tips. They were a list of nearly a hundred items we gradually whittled down to fifty-two that we felt would have the most impact on coffee shop owners.

The second book was different. *The Coffee Boys' Step-by-step Guide to Setting Up and Managing Your Own Coffee Bar: How to open a coffee bar that actually lasts and makes money*, was much more of a process (detailed on page 7) for how owners and managers could systematically work through our methods and make their businesses not just more profitable but also better places to work for both the owners and their employees.

Both books were a great success and since the publication of the second we have worked with hundreds of owners and managers to help put this process in place in their businesses – either through coaching and consulting or via our online courses. Additionally, we've helped grow several businesses in preparation for a sale – spectacularly so in one case – and built a chain, from scratch, which now has more than twenty-three outlets.

But . . . there's a problem with that. It creates complacency, a belief that one knows it all, that actually there is very little that we can learn or be taught.

It leads to a slightly odd phenomenon, that you are undoubtedly familiar with, called 'confirmation bias'. If you go to that great resource out there in the ether – Wikipedia – you find the following definition:

> **Confirmation bias**, also called **myside bias**, is the tendency to search for, interpret or recall information in a way that confirms one's beliefs or hypotheses. It is a type of cognitive bias and a systematic error of inductive reasoning. People display this bias when they gather or remember information selectively, or when they interpret it in a biased way. The effect is stronger for emotionally charged issues and for deeply entrenched beliefs. People also tend to interpret ambiguous evidence as supporting their existing position.

Confirmation bias, as well as the myriad other cognitive biases, is something we all need to be very careful of. Hugh and I see it in various forms in nearly all the businesses we work with. In short, it involves people thinking that their view of the world is right, and searching, whether consciously or not, for evidence to back this up.

It's absolutely rife in the hospitality business, especially with startups. Which is why we'll always push clients to seek and work with data-driven decisions, i.e. hard, measurable facts. This is the core of how we initially measure where a business is, and subsequently how effective any change management has been.

Ultimately, what you or I, your mum, your staff, your best friend, Hugh, your suppliers or any other expert thinks is irrelevant if the till reading tells us, at the end of the week, that the customer doesn't like what we've created. That's what matters. Customers either like what you do or they don't – what you think about it is irrelevant.

With that in mind we chose to write this new book in a very specific way. We decided to ask the owners, operators and senior managers of some of the best coffee shops and cafés in the world two simple questions:

1. **What is the one thing you wish you'd known before you started?**

2. **What do you believe is the secret to success of your business and great coffee shops and cafés in general?**

But there is one critical issue to bear in mind here. We made sure that we didn't guide our contributors in any way and that there was as little referring back to our material as possible. We wanted the honest truth. What we didn't want was a book that confirmed our belief that our material was perfect and correct in every way.

To a large extent it didn't matter if the answers confirmed or slightly conflicted with our formula. If they confirmed it, we could continue to march forth and help clients with a stronger sense of conviction that, within a very complex industry, we really did have the solution. The exact formula for success.

If the answers conflicted, in any way, with what we said, we could amend our formula and processes to take this into account and incorporate it into our future coaching, consulting and courses.

For us, and hopefully for you, the reader, there was no downside – whatever the outcome of our research, we'd end up several steps closer to a perfect model for the creation of a great coffee shop or café.

To help support and round out this research we, along with the wonderful Caffè Culture organisation, also produced a large piece of research that would extend well beyond the individual answers within this book. We wanted that research to reinforce (or not) the thoughts and ideas contained within these pages.

That piece of research has grown into something of a monster and we're close to having detailed answers from 10 per cent of the UK's independent coffee shop operators and a good chunk from the rest of the world too.

To access the full research findings and our interpretation of them, make sure you visit www.wakeupandsellbook.com.

Within this book, though, we wanted the very best that we could find. We rejected some potential candidates because, although they appeared superficially successful, they weren't making money. That was our only bias. This book isn't a coffee shop 'the good, the bad and the ugly' – it's just the good. It has input from owners who will almost certainly have had a bit of bad and ugly along the way but who have now finally got their businesses to work. Who have, to use our consulting and coaching terminology, put all the pieces of the jigsaw together.

Initially, we also aspired to get as many of the big chains involved as we could. From our own perspective that would have been great. Big names equals more publicity equals more books sold for wee Johnny and Hugo. But we rejected that because when we started down that route, the banal and obviously PR-driven responses were of little or no use.

So, at the time of writing, there is no chain with more than fifty sites included and there are multiple highly successful single-site operators. It's also an eclectic mix of people. We have World and UK barista champions rubbing shoulders with investment bankers and ex-plumbers. We've got a Seattle-based legend that arguably helped create the industry as we know it today (and I'm not referring to Howard Schultz). We've got some of the most respected suppliers in the world – all of whom have dipped their toes into ownership at some stage, too.

Without wishing to repeat myself too much, these responses are in their words. And only at the end will we review and see how it all fits into our seven-step formula for success and what the main takeaways are.

I read several years ago, conveniently before we wrote our first book, that 95 per cent of business books are never read past the first chapter. I'd be lying if I said I'm not in that category fairly often myself.

That's why we've always attempted to write books that can be dipped in and out of without the feel of a school textbook. To that end we've included our side stories with each interview and a one-sentence takeaway that will hopefully help you apply the wisdom of each contributor in a concise way.

In my slightly needy writer way though, I really would urge that you read all the contributions. There is some brilliant insight and a huge amount that you can directly apply to your own business – or a potential startup if you've yet to open.

THE GREAT FORMULA

If you haven't read our second book (*The Coffee Boys' Step-by-step Guide to Setting Up and Managing Your Own Coffee Bar*) or attended any of our courses, here is a brief summary of our formula for success. This is, in effect, the process or the rules, the validity of which we're testing with this book.

Note: I deliberately re-wrote this formula before we started interviewing and did not edit it to fit the responses when the process was complete.

1. Passion – To be a success in this industry you must have a passionate desire to serve great food and drink. If you come in purely for the money (or some misguided notion that there is easy money to be made) then you will be painfully let down.

In the future, the process for creating great food and drink will undoubtedly be increasingly automated, but right now people are buying much more than a generic cup of coffee and a sandwich when they visit you.

And don't forget this business is tough – you must have that passion to keep going when the inevitable difficulties hit.

2. Product (or Taste) – Obsessional passion produces great tasting products. If you're not driven by a passionate vision to be the best, then you'll cut corners with ingredients. Staff won't worry so much about presentation. You'll start to listen to the salesman selling you the cheaper and easier way to make substitutes and you'll even believe that 'the customer will never notice'.

Trust me – the customer will always notice. You simply cannot expect to succeed in this game if your starting point is 'good enough is good enough'.

3. Positioning – Put very simply, you must have the right product for the right market. A high-end espresso bar selling premium, 85 per cent cocoa brownies won't survive beside the builders' merchants, and the bacon sandwich and mug of tea café won't work alongside the slickest advertising agencies in Soho. And if you expect customers to wait ten minutes for a perfect coffee and scone at your train station kiosk in the morning, you won't survive long.

It's common sense, but all too often we find coffee shop owners frustrated that their customers won't buy what they're selling, simply because the owners haven't read their market properly. Everything you do in your business must be driven through the shoes, eyes and needs of the customers that will be passing by.

4. People – Trying to summarise the people part of the formula in a couple of paragraphs is utterly pointless. We produce full-day seminars on each of the following: recruitment, induction training, staff retention, management training, and leadership. The leadership training is actually two days long – that's how important people are in the whole equation.

To keep it simple, think of your business like this – a coffee shop or café is about people employing people, serving people. Once you have the food and beverage aspect sorted, that's what you need to focus on.

5. Systems – So now we have our great food, great coffee, passionate leadership, expert recruiting and we're developing great people – how do we hold it all together?

Systems.

A business is run by systems and people run the systems.

Without crystal-clear systems and processes you create a business that confuses employees and can never provide a consistent experience for your customer. The one advantage that the big chains have over you is their operational systems and the ability to deliver a consistent service. Make sure you remove that advantage.

6. Marketing – If there's one battle cry that Hugh and I have often heard over the years which frustrates us the most it's: 'The business is great – we just need to do some marketing'. 90 per cent of the time this is incorrect. What we find is evidence of owner confirmation bias in place and that, quite frankly, the business is NOT great. The offer isn't good enough and the staff are not performing as they should.

If you spend money driving people to a business that hasn't got the first five steps in the formula in place, then it's simply wasted money. Customers will arrive, be disappointed and not return.

But once you have the business properly sorted, of course it is vital that you do keep marketing. And never forget that marketing is never just about getting new customers – what is at least as important is ensuring those that do visit provide you with a high average spend and that they return frequently.

7. Money – Now you've got to make sure it all hangs together. You've got to know your figures. You need to make sure that on a weekly (or at most monthly) basis you know exactly how much, or how little, you've made.

You've got to know, to the penny, what everything on the menu costs.

So, that's the formula, or should I say *our* formula, for success in a coffee shop. That's it at its most simple. In reality, of course, it is nothing like as simple as that. For our online coaching group this formula is broken down into dozens of forms, templates, documents, videos and training modules.

And it really works. Using this formula we have created a turn-key, multi-site coffee business from scratch, with every site making money from day one. It has helped a government body reduce spending by £2 million per year. It has formed the basis of decisions made by venture capitalists and grown businesses to a level where they sell for income multiples well beyond the industry norms.

To see a much fuller explanation of how we use this formula, check out the bonus material at www.wakeupandsellbook.com.

But . . . this book is about seeing exactly how other great coffee shops work. It's about seeing what their secrets are, what processes they follow on a day-to-day basis to ensure success.

So that's how we arrived at the two big questions that form the basis of this book. And at the end, we'll compare and contrast and discover the commonalities between how we work and how these 'best in the industry' operators work.

THE TWO BIG QUESTIONS – AND OUR OWN ANSWERS

Before we move on to the answers provided by twenty-two owners, operators and senior managers of some of the best coffee shops and cafés in the world, Hugh and I wrote our own versions of how we would answer the questions. Since it's our book, we took a few liberties and perhaps bent the rules slightly, but our thinking and scribblings represent a further six years of work within the industry – some of it at a very high level – beyond what we said in our last book.

JOHNNY RICHARDSON

When we created our first question, we knew the concept of 'one thing' was really there to provide focus but that it also begs to be abused. For any businessperson with any decent length of career it's almost impossible to distil any solution or answer down to 'one thing'.

Last year my daughter was undertaking business studies for her GCSEs and she asked me how many businesses I'd owned.

The answer surprised me: nineteen.

That's not nineteen different units within a few businesses – it's nineteen distinct businesses. So my sandwich business with its multiple sites and a factory counts as one. As do the garden centres. So really, by any definition of the word, I'm an entrepreneur. A serial entrepreneur, even.

When I was at university completing my business studies degree in the late eighties, the word entrepreneur had an almost dirty feel to it.

I can remember Shane MacGowan from The Pogues snarling about brass in the pocket of an entrepreneur in their wonderful song about Irish navvies – 'Navigator'.

Within that context, an entrepreneur wasn't something I wanted to be. It seemed to be something very negative, exploitative even. Nineteen businesses later, though, it's hard to deny that's what I am. But thankfully the connotations of the word appear to have changed – as has my slightly 'right-on' naiveté surrounding it. It seems these days entrepreneurialism is something to be celebrated. A good thing – a way to grow the economy and help provide people with work that really resonates with them.

If you've read anything I've written before, you'll know that it hasn't all been plain sailing – it never is – but during that period of time I've employed more than 1000 people and paid a huge amount of tax. I've also experienced the pain and humiliation of business collapse.

And I've known a lot of friends go through the same, especially within Ireland in the last few years. Business is tough and lots of people don't make it, but in this book we've pulled together a wonderful selection of owners and operators who have. A few of them have been burned along the way but right now they're all successful.

So that's my long-winded way of justifying why I didn't just name 'one thing'. And I'm not alone in this: a large number of our interviewees couldn't keep their answer to a single idea either – I have no issue with that. What we really wanted was a collection of critical issues that successful business owners felt should be focused on.

What is the one thing you wish you'd known before you started?

So, with that context in mind, here are the 'one things' I wish I'd known about:

1. Total responsibility – I've talked about this before, but it cannot be overemphasised. It's so important, in fact, that I'm halfway through an entire book (albeit a short business fable) on this very subject. In my early twenties, when I was starting my first 'proper' businesses, I simply didn't get this. I was far too quick to blame locations, staff, the economy, my partners, anything really. What I did have though, was the confidence, energy and enthusiasm of youth. That counts for a lot. If you can have a moan and then bounce out of bed the next day to give it another go, then a certain lack of responsibility can be ignored.

But older managers and owners don't have that luxury. The desire to blame others can eat away like cancer if you're tired and worn down by debt, the need to put food on the table and keep a roof over your family's heads. An inability to take responsibility and no energy is an almost guaranteed formula for failure.

I learnt the lesson the hard way. After my first business collapsed there were myriad available excuses that allowed me, and my business partner at the time, to not shoulder much of the blame. But a very serious talking-to by an older and very successful business friend put me straight.

Teaching total responsibility for your business or the site that you manage still rests at the very core of any management or leadership training I do. So ignore it at your peril.

2. Check your ego – I'm afraid to say I'm one of those fools who sometimes has to make the same mistake twice. I've expanded businesses into multiple sites more than once, before I'd entirely 'finished' the first one and ensured it was profitable and highly systemised. I'd be lying if I said this wasn't ego driven. It's not, however, a mistake I'll make again. Honestly.

14

3. Get a proper mentor or business coach – If you're going to grow any business properly you need to make sure there is someone there who is experienced enough and wise enough to say: '*Hold on there fella, why exactly are you doing that?*' It took me a long time to find these types of people, but I now meet with various groups and mentors and make certain that the vast majority of them are more successful than I am.

This 'one thing' would undoubtedly have saved my sandwich business from collapse.

What do you believe is the secret to success of your business and great coffee shops and cafés in general?

If I step back and think beyond our formula (which is actually quite tough to do these days since it forms the backbone of all our work), the following spring to mind:

1. An obsessive concern for the customer – This is perhaps the biggest and simplest secret. The really great guys are constantly thinking about what their customers want, what they're experiencing, what will make them stay and which competitor might make them stray. It's a process that must permeate the very core of the business via recruitment and training. It cannot just come from the owner.

2. Really great food and drink and a curiosity to keep improving – Hugh and I often talk about great coffee being the price of entry these days, but often that isn't actually the case. There's still a lot of rubbish coffee out there and some pretty shocking food. The greats not only provide great food and drink today

15

but are on a constant quest to improve and create new menu items to excite/tempt/delight (choose your own cliché) the customer.

3. Creating systems that run the business and then recruiting people to run the systems – This starts with great clarity of vision. What do you actually want the business to look like? How exactly will it serve the customer? Once you have this in place (and that can and should take some time), you create systems and processes to ensure that every single detail of this is covered. Finally, you recruit, train and develop people to share this vision and put these systems in place.

4. The greats know their numbers – Absolutely no doubt about it. No matter how creative the owner may feel they are, or how great a level of artistry goes into their food or coffee, they know their numbers. And the really brilliant ones have a dedicated measurement dashboard in place to ensure the key metrics – some of which may not even be financial – are measured and reported on in a systematic and very regular fashion.

HUGH GILMARTIN

As we collaborate on this our third book, a lot of water has already passed under the bridge and the coffee business has changed almost beyond recognition. The high street coffee-bar market has doubled in size and the independent sector has gone through second, third and fourth waves to deliver quality and experiences that are better than ever. The economy continues to dictate decisions in this very marginal business sector, and only those that are very good can actually build sustainable and valuable brands.

As a supplier, advisor and consultant, selling knowledge products has become more difficult and challenging because so many people believe that information, advice and expertise should be transferred in preliminary meetings at no cost. Also, there is so much content out there that at times it feels there is just too much and that everybody is an expert.

Certainly it is very easy to qualify information using a simple Google search and that too is a symptom that defines a deeper business problem – which is that we have to be far more selective about what we do and, more importantly, who we work with. Trust, an abused word in business, has become the key to successful outcomes. When it is high things get done faster and at less cost; when it is low everything suffers and long-term relationships are impossible.

What does excite me working in the business of creating and executing high-end coffee experiences is that we are engaged in changing behaviour and helping people move towards what is desired by carefully identifying what outcomes we want. Doing this with the right people is rewarding, challenging, in some cases explosive, and always great fun.

It has been fantastic working through the many brilliant responses in this book and realising how wise some of the points are and how useful some of the ideas will be to me. For me, the realisation that we are always learning is right there in front of me when I read a book like this. Putting it together has been a great experience and my gratitude goes to all of the friends, clients and acquaintances that we have included – as well as to many of those we didn't!

What is the one thing you wish you'd known before you started?

I am deeply involved now in change management of many businesses and organisations. That is because those people I work with want to know the models we have used successfully to transform situations. Generally the way it works is they decide if it will work for them and basically we then execute an agreed plan that has measured outcomes; we also make each other accountable.

The one thing I wish I'd known clearly at the start is what I now know for sure: that it's always my fault if I don't achieve success, because it will have been my choice to work with a particular client. I am sometimes asked, 'Can somebody change the way they behave' and the obvious answer is, 'Yes of course', but most of us need to hurt in order to change; it won't happen just because somebody suggests it. So if certain circumstances or barriers mean you can't change the situation, then I say 'change your attitude towards it'. If someone is miserable, that's up to them: their responsibility, their participation, their choice. You can always choose to be positive.

I think this is the one concept that if I was young and starting again I would focus on like a laser: That **I am responsible** (able to respond) for every outcome.

What do you believe is the secret to success of your business and great coffee shops and cafés in general?

This is one of those questions that sounds like a great question (it is!) and is very difficult to answer. It's because of the language apart from everything else – we all know that in reality there's no such thing as a secret to success. For me, however, there are fundamental strategies and concepts that I have learnt from other people and worked with over the years that have made fantastic differences; the one reality that goes with these fundamentals is that they only work if you actually do them.

The other thought I have around a question like this is that many people have given answers that have worked for, resonated with and also failed in their respective businesses, and they are all correct – because everything you execute depends on you. So from that perspective I am listing six (the above answer to the first question is the seventh) fundamental ideas that I think have been highly useful, and have worked for me and others in the operation and execution of running coffee bars and many related businesses.

Individual leadership. It's always crucial to identify the leader. This is not necessarily the manager, and in many cases the leader is not a good manager. But all businesses need a clear vision and an ideal that once you have properly identified and clarified, you work back from to decide what to do this week.

Modelling. A basic fundamental of NLP (neuro-linguistic programming), this concept effectively says that if you can identify a process that works well for somebody, then you can model that to work for you; we all do it to a greater or lesser degree.

Tell the truth. There is so much fake marketing in today's world. Everybody is the best and marketing copy screams faster, cheaper, stronger, bigger, better. For example, everyone says their coffee is fantastic and many have no idea how to control the process to prepare every cup to within a consistent target. The main reason for this is because telling the truth costs money; the biggest issue is that businesses often cut costs because they decide that the customer can't tell the difference. Corners are cut and the lie is that they don't change the story they are telling. The reality is that nobody actually cares enough to challenge this because in the consumer's mind, there is no credibility there to start with. There is far too much manipulation going on in today's world; however, much of it is obvious if you know how to spot it.

Customer shoes. Ultimately this concept, carried out properly, has delivered for me probably the best, consistent small scores and results over the years. It means having a very heightened awareness of other people's points of view and thinking, and also careful listening strategies built into the business to enable the gathering of the necessary information to make data-validated decisions. It is also probably the most important communication tool in helping you persuade anybody to see things your way. Determining the other person's position, priorities, perceptions and prejudices before you try to get them to agree with you makes such a difference and it is not an easy or quick thing to do.

Sensuality. Applying the senses in a systemised way to situations, projects, designs, marketing, sales, buildings and people can take you to different levels of experiences and solutions. Consider carefully what things look, sound, taste, smell and feel like. Get more than three right simultaneously and you are in the money!

Numbers. Everything is measured in numbers and the better your ability to first, identify what numbers you need every week and second, have the discipline to ensure your business has in place systems and processes to report those numbers in a like-for-like basis, the better your life will be; this is the single biggest 'secret' that I suggest will make the most difference to your business. And the proper numbers never lie. You just have to discover how to get them! A final benefit of knowing the numbers is that you can then identify fairly quickly 'What's the worst that can happen?' – and asking that question helps you make the difficult daily decisions that somebody has to do for growth to happen. And if you are not growing you are going backwards.

And my final recommendation is to turn up on time, do what you say and finish what you start. It's as easy – and as difficult – as that!

22 ANSWERS TO THE TWO BIG QUESTIONS

BEN TOWNSEND

The Espresso Room Café

One of the most experienced barista trainers in the UK, Ben was a member of the original panel that developed the City & Guilds VRQ Barista qualification. He is the proprietor of The Espresso Room Café in Bloomsbury, London, which has received outstanding reviews. His training technique has been developed from years of experience both as a high-end barista and, importantly, running his own businesses.

www.theespressoroom.com

What is the one thing you wish you'd known before you started?

There's a very short answer to this: numbers. It seems ridiculous now, but I had never heard of things like gross profit or net margin. I always thought that other people knew what they were doing, but in those days, in specialty coffee in London, it turned out that we were all copying each other on price. None of us had done COGs or GP calculations. Unfortunately, this set the template for price across all the dozens of subsequent cafés that opened up, so most London specialty cafés were as cheap, or even cheaper, than the chains, but with much higher costs.

In my opinion, this one mistake has rippled out across UK specialty with pretty depressing consequences – low staff wages, low owner profit and little budget for innovation and development. I constantly warn people on my barista courses to pay attention to this stuff. The prices that you see in chain coffee stores, or in regular non-specialty cafés, may or may not be correct for those types of business, but they are certainly not correct for the specialty model.

High-quality coffee, machinery, milk and baristas cost more (and they should!). Plus, of course, you are going to pay your VAT and corporation tax (lots of cafés don't). You need to build all that into your business model and pricing structure.

What do you believe is the secret to success of your business and great coffee shops and cafés in general?

The secret is no secret – it's wanting to do it.

It's perfectly OK to say that you don't like standing all day, or working seventy-hour weeks. It's perfectly OK to say that you like going on lots of holidays, or working quietly on your own. But that should lead you to some other job. Coffee is a 'hospitality' job, and hospitality is an inherently physically and mentally demanding industry. But if you have the personality and constitution to do it, then the rewards are great.

You have to genuinely want to provide service to everybody who walks through the door. You have to create an environment for your staff to thrive and learn – they will reward you for it. It's there to see in every great café, restaurant, bar or whatever.

You can feel it instantly – if it feels right, it almost certainly is.

JOHNNY – SIDE STORY

Ben's answer to 'the one thing' is the very reason Hugh and I wrote *Wake Up and Smell the Profit* in the style that we did. If you haven't read it (shame on you), we wrote fifty-three short chapters, or tips, on running coffee shops better. But the first three chapters were entitled 'It's all about the money 1', 'It's all about the money 2' and 'It's all about the money 3'.

I expected to get more flak for that. But thankfully it never came – the message we were desperate to get across is that a huge majority of entrants into this industry simply have no solid grasp of the numbers and of concepts like gross and net profit. Or fixed and variable costs.

Many entrants, despite our best efforts with books, seminars and coaching and the work we do with Caffè Culture, still open up and assume they will make money simply by copying prices and making an exceptional cup of coffee.

Ben Townsend's one-sentence takeaway
Create an environment in which your staff can thrive and learn – they will reward you for it (and know your numbers . . .).

CARL SARA

Crafted Coffee Company

From Christchurch, New Zealand, Crafted Coffee Company was founded by four times New Zealand Barista Champion Carl Sara. Coffee competitions and fifteen years owning cafés has provided Carl with the unique opportunity to travel extensively internationally, participating in and observing many of the coffee world's different levels. He has been chair of World Coffee Events Advisory Board and is very well known in the global coffee community. He is the immediate past president for the board of the New Zealand Specialty Coffee Association.

www.craftedcoffeecompany.co.nz

What is the one thing you wish you'd known before you started?

This is difficult to answer because there is not only one thing. What I would say is that not running a coffee shop as a coffee shop but rather as a 'business that is a coffee shop' is up there as the one thing. So often we see people doing things that are innovative, ground-breaking and challenging within the coffee sector, buts it's really important not to lose sight of the fact that it's a business.

What do you believe is the secret to success of your business and great coffee shops and cafés in general?

I started by buying a franchise in 1999 because it had a good P&L. I wouldn't say that I was in any way a coffee expert or getting into it for the love of coffee. I saw it as a way to make money. Entering barista competitions didn't come from a romantic idea either. I thought it was a good marketing tool to sell more coffee. It was only when I got involved in competing and all that goes with it that it hit me – and the whole world of coffee opened up for me. As I have learnt more, and realised there is always more to learn about coffee, my passion and commitment to the industry grows.

Looking back now I would have to say that one of the key issues is to understand that your business as a brand is so much about the people, because it is the team that makes your brand. Your duty is to provide a platform for staff to grow and flourish. I have heard many complain that they have trained and invested in people only for them to leave, whereas I have the view that if that happens to us then so be it. You should never be afraid of staff leaving and growing. All the best guys in the business have come through employee to boss and employer roles: just think of Colin Harmon, James Hoffman, Stephen Morrissey, Michael Phillips and many more. You have to be known for promoting and positioning good people and this investment does eventually come full circle.

Two other things occur to me with this question:

One, we are based in Christchurch, and as everybody knows, we have gone through turmoil over the past few years with the earthquake. As a result of that particular disaster, the market has evolved at an incredible rate; it has been a rollercoaster ride of originally having many coffee bars, cafés and restaurants to only a few, post-earthquake, and now again many, as the insurance claims come through. We have had ten years' growth in two or three years and you have to constantly evolve, be nimble and act very quickly on calculated instinct. You have to think about what can happen, assess the pluses and minuses of the situation and then just do it.

The other thing is to identify what your business is and needs to be in *your* marketplace and then innovate to achieve that vision. What works in Dublin, London or Milan may not be what works in New Zealand. Five or six years ago for example, New Zealand was very fashionable and trendy in London and we did manage to be a significant influence in the city, but that may not be the case today. You have to interpret how it will work locally for you.

HUGO – SIDE STORY

Carl Sara is an entrepreneur first and then a coffee expert in every way. Sourcing, roasting, brewing, training, wholesaling and retailing – he covers every base, and brilliantly. This is a key part of his success. He also knows exactly what he wants and is generous with his time and knowledge. His story about using barista competitions to sell more coffee in the early days resonates so much with me, as I remember when I first started selling coffee as a rep ordering it black – because I thought it would make it look like I knew more about coffee. I didn't even like coffee in those days; you can imagine the quality of black coffee I had to endure, so it's no wonder. Then, like Carl, the whole coffee world opened up with a few key experiences. Crafted Coffee Company in Christchurch is 100 per cent on my bucket list.

JOHNNY – SIDE STORY

Carl's interview fascinates me – to an outsider he is purely a coffee man, but his point about making sure that your coffee shop is a business first and foremost is something that should be etched on the mirror of every owner or potential owner in the world.

Secondly, his final paragraph about positioning is critical. Business consultants of old used to preach about how you could take something that was working well in one country and simply replicate it in your own to be guaranteed success. The example, oft quoted, was frozen yoghurt bars – when did you last see one of those?

The critical point is that you must know your market in great detail and how to position your offering. There simply is no 'one size fits all' where coffee shops and food businesses in general are concerned. That's not to say you can't take great ideas and elements from other countries and test them in your market, but they must be taken with a very good understanding of the local geography and purchasing habits of your local area.

Carl Sara's one-sentence takeaway
Your duty is to provide a platform in your business for staff to grow and flourish. Never be afraid of them leaving you, and their value will always stay with your business.

DARREN GARDINER

Ground Espresso

Darren started Ground from a single site on the north coast of Ireland in 2001. Since then he has built a chain with fourteen sites and continues to expand rapidly both on high street locations and through some innovative link-ups with major retailers in retail parks. Ground is an exceptional example of a coffee-shop chain positioned well within its marketplace.

www.groundcoffee.net

What is the one thing you wish you'd known before you started?

I wish I'd known just how hard it is to make it in the coffee industry!

I hear weekly of someone who wants to open a coffee bar and so many times I want to grab them, shake them and scream, 'Are you sure you want to do this?' It's a tough business to be in and if you want to succeed you need to forget everything you think you know about the industry and do some serious research.

If you're doing it as a lifestyle choice, you'll love it. If you're doing it because someone told you you'll get rich, you'll be disappointed and your partner will moan at you for always smelling of coffee.

What do you believe is the secret to success of your business and great coffee shops and cafés in general?

Three things!

Attention to detail. You need to analyse and dissect every little detail of your business. You need to constantly strive for perfection but also understand that you'll never quite get there, that there will always be things you know aren't quite right (back to attention to detail)! You also need to look carefully at what's on-trend. You need to know what people want and you need to know if it will work in your geographical area. Just because something is on-trend in Shoreditch, it does not mean it will work in Inverness. A good example of this was the trend towards cold brewed coffee last season – great in London, but you couldn't give it away in rural Ireland!

There are a lot more housewives than hipsters. You don't need a beard, flatcap and several piercings to make it in the industry. Good coffee should be accessible to all. We need to drop this elitist crap and as an industry strive to improve coffee standards across the board.

Be original. It's sad to see everyone doing the same thing. If you've built your business off the back of someone else's ideas you'll always be one step behind. Take chances and put energy and resources into research and development. As a business we invest heavily in this and it's money well spent.

JOHNNY – SIDE STORY

Darren doesn't mention it, but he also owns and runs a very successful audiovisual company. This business means that Darren travels a lot and is away from Ground on a regular basis. So when he talks about attention to detail he really means it – you simply cannot grow a business as fast and effectively as Darren is doing without a meticulous level of control over what is going on.

Darren Gardiner's one-sentence takeaway
Positioning – make sure you know and understand your local marketplace at an instinctive level.

DAVID SCHOMER

Espresso Vivace

There are few genuine legends in this industry (plenty in their own minds though . . .), but David is certainly one. He is the owner of Vivace, which he established with his partner Geneva Sullivan in 1988. They operate three cafés in Seattle. He is also the author of *Espresso Coffee*, which was first published in 1995. This book has been revised several times and is now available in Japanese, Russian and Korean. David has also produced multiple highly influential video trainings.

David kindly let us interview him by Skype and the full video, along with the transcripts, is available in the supporting material (see page ix).

http://espressovivace.com

What is the one thing you wish you'd known before you started?

The thing that I wish I'd known before I started the business is that if you want your staff to do artistic work, it requires a customer that's sensitive to experience and flavours.

What happened to us was we opened at 5th and Union in 1989 and one year later I opened at 301 Broadway Avenue East. Down at 5th and Union, the majority of the residents were in the financial industry in one way or another, and I couldn't build any loyalty. One day they'd come by and say, 'Oh, this is the best thing I ever had' and then the next day they'd have a Starbucks; the day after that they'd have an SBC – there was absolutely no interest in having a better cup.

This made my staff very frustrated. They didn't want to work there. I had all kinds of problems and ended up almost losing the company before I convinced my wife at the time, Geneva, that we'd got it wrong. I said, 'This was a big mistake opening at 5th and Union because the people are not sensitive to culinary experience.'

So, the other thing I could offer is that if people are going to do artistic coffee, and they would like their staff to be able to reproduce what they do with enthusiasm, staff need to have some artistry in their nature. Obviously they are all people persons. They're all very excited about making the customer happy. That's what we do first and foremost, but some customers just aren't able to make staff happy, and those people will wear you down. If you have customers that don't care about what they drink or, even worse, like to be abusive to customer service professionals, it is the kiss of death for a gourmet business – it won't work for the staff; any effort they put in is not going to be appreciated.

So I closed 5th and Union after two years of a very frustrating experience. Then I came up to Broadway. I opened the Roasteria Vivace at 901 E. Denny Way, and I had my cart; here the customers were so appreciative of what we do.

To refine it even further, Roasteria Vivace was near a community college, and the community college students would come in, but they didn't know any better. I mean if you're putting out art and you don't have competitors around or people that have experienced coffee for a number of years, they have no idea how good you are. It was a good crowd, but that was seized from me under eminent domain [the power of state or government to take private property for public use] in 2006. Our lease was broken so they could build a transit station.

Well, I moved that shop five blocks north to 532 Broadway Avenue East, where you are surrounded by what I would call high-end housing for a three-mile radius. These people are all between thirty and sixty or seventy and they are really savvy. They appreciate what we do and they are just rabidly loyal. OK, so I had to learn that if you do art on one side of the counter, it has to exist on the other side too.

What do you believe is the secret to success of your business and of great coffee shops and cafés in general?

The secret to success is that owners understand passion. They all start with passion, but all business is so tough that it must be at the absolute core of who you really are. I was lucky to find out that I was that person.

I was interested, passionately interested, in making a better cup, and twenty-six years later, when I look back, I realise the absolute fidelity that I have to that idea. I'm trying to express a humble thought here that it was eye-opening, and I was glad to find out that that's who I truly am. I am absolutely not going to expand [the business]. I keep my focus on perfection and we do a lot of business.

Now the other part of that success story is the other owner, Geneva. You must have a competent numbers' person – somebody that's looking at and paying all the taxes, helping to adjust prices based on an accurate view of the cost of goods sold, and also knows where the money is. Most businesses fail either because they don't pay their taxes or they have some other regulatory problem, or they don't know where the money is. Often they simply don't understand how much it costs to build up that cup of coffee.

My long-time partner – we're no longer married, but we're very good business and parent partners – Geneva Sullivan, is my secret weapon. I have seen a lot of people come in with my passion and get ground down because of some mistake they make. Geneva prevents me, and Espresso Vivace, from making those mistakes.

Conversely – and I don't know why coffee is so affected this way – but almost everybody that starts out in the States (I won't name names, but one of them has this artisan reputation and a big name), has made the same mistake of opening multiple stores before they have high-integrity managers in place that are thoroughly vetted and know what they're doing.

Vivace has resisted expansion because of my nature. I will not spend my time in an office or talking to bankers, doing all this expansion stuff, trying to train people fifty at a time, any of this crap. I train one by one.

I'm small and focused because it's my nature. I can't help it. That's what I have to do. I have to continue to perfect this. And so it's the team – it's the fidelity of me, the founder, imagination and creator of the coffee, and Geneva, the one who is going to sit there and make damned sure we're profitable and understands where every penny is. She just recently came up with a new analysis to discover if we had any sort of problems with staffing, a brilliant financial analysis but which is a little bit on the dark side.

Now what happens when the owner has the passion and it's real is that the people that come to work for you, at least in the States, are very excited and they are truly involved in what we say because it's real. It's what they see in me every day. If the grinder needs work it happens that second. It doesn't happen a week later, with: 'Oh, no problem. We'll get to that.' I'm not marketing. I'm not doing that. What I'm doing is exactly what I said: I'm focused 100 per cent and I'm innovating all the time.

JOHNNY – SIDE STORY

David Schomer changed my life with respect to understanding coffee and the detail required to produce it well. To a large extent he changed my understanding of business way beyond the production of a great cup of coffee.

I bought my first espresso machine in 1995 and spent the next few years producing what can only be described as truly shocking coffee. In fairness to me, in Northern Ireland, the market, which David so eloquently talks about in his responses, simply wasn't aware of what great coffee could be at that stage. When people asked for an expresso (sic) what they meant, most of the time was a cappuccino. So when we handed them a badly produced espresso, they were shocked, not by how bad it was but because they'd wanted a coffee with a big frothy, milky top.

When I met Hugh and I was opening my next ventures into coffee, I was still very sceptical about the need to spend a lot of time and money on equipment and training. I thought we could consider rolling out poor coffee and making 'an easy buck'.

In a frustrated fashion, Hugh handed me a video (old-school VHS) and told me to go home and watch it. Such was the arrogance of youth that I ignored him. After he'd asked me several times what I thought of it and then told me how much he'd paid for it (approximately 80 dollars, I believe) I decided to give it a chance. The video was short, not particularly well lit and I sincerely doubted that I was going to learn anything.

That video was of David Schomer showing how he made a perfect espresso and the systems and processes he had in place in his business to ensure that happened. To say I was shocked was an understatement. The passion and attention to detail that David talks about is not part of a cheap marketing message. The training processes that his staff go through has to be seen to be believed.

It's a lesson I've attempted to take into every food and beverage business I've owned or advised since then. And I heartily recommend that you follow David's work and absorb some of that passion for detail into your own business.

HUGO – SIDE STORY

Anybody lucky enough to have been trained by David knows it. He talks about the necessity for passion (which I believe is an abused word in business) because people rarely exhibit the attitude that is real passion. David taught me what great coffee should taste like and helped us create good coffee in Ireland because we introduced the double ristretto shot base and reinvented cappuccinos in the Nineties.

Of course today we are all at a different level, but back then it was truly innovative and made a massive difference to my customers' profits – quite simply, their coffee tasted better because we used David's fundamental preparation rules around recipe and grind as you go. It took ten years for grinder manufacturers to listen and produce portion-controlled, on-demand conical grinders.

David was a wonderful influence on my business and he is a unique character who, in my view, is a legend. Definitely different, usually intense when it comes to coffee outcomes, and always worth listening very carefully to.

David Schomer's one-sentence takeaway

Never let your passion for producing a truly exceptional product falter, but make sure that it is always grounded in sound business and financial sense.

DEVINDER DHALLU

Six Eight Kafé

Devinder is the owner of Six Eight Kafé in Birmingham – voted one of the top 50 coffee shops in the UK by the *Independent*. Recently, he opened a second, much larger site. Don't be surprised if you see Devinder as a major player in the industry during the coming decade.

www.sixeightkafe.co.uk

What is the one thing you wish you'd known before you started?

A. That it is not just about making a great cup of coffee. I learnt this from you guys but it really didn't sink in until much later on. You can make a great cup of coffee, but nobody will know about it unless you let them know. You need to be a great marketer as well as producer of a great cup of coffee.

B. When you open a coffee shop, you are in fact opening a business. So you need to know all aspects of a business (finance, systems, marketing, staff etc.).

C. You have to become a different person when opening a coffee shop/business. The skills you needed whilst working for somebody else will not be enough when you open a business. You will need to develop your mind-set as well as the skillset specific to a coffee shop

D. You need a lot more money than you think to keep you going through the first few years.

What do you believe is the secret to success of your business and great coffee shops and cafés in general?

For a coffee shop, I would say the following are the secrets to success:

Marketing. We constantly market ourselves, all of the time. As well as using social media, we regularly send press releases and they always seem to get published, sometimes word for word. I learnt about press releases from you guys. Whenever any national publication asks for an opinion/input, I always reply. They in turn publish news about us.

Courage. We are physically a small shop and should really be daunted by entering national barista championships, which are dominated by large roasters, but we have reached the semi-finals twice in three years.

Staff. We have been blessed over the years with great staff. Unfortunately, we are in an industry which has a high turnover of staff, so we have to constantly find new staff. But we are fortunate in that we always find great new staff.

Owner. I know this may sound cocky, but the ultimately the success/failure rests with the owner. His vision, confidence, mind-set, determination, staff management and financial knowledge play a huge part in the outcome of business.

JOHNNY – SIDE STORY

When Hugh and I first started our Coffee Boys experiment, nearly ten years ago, we did a one-hour talk at Caffè Culture. Thankfully it went very well and a number of people came up to ask us questions afterwards.

A young and enthusiastic young man, going by the name of Devinder Dhallu, was one of them.

Since then, it seems as though for every book, every talk and every paid seminar we've undertaken Devinder has continued to be there. But unlike some others, Devinder worked extremely hard, and implemented and put together a great business. When his business was featured on breakfast TV I felt like a proud uncle!

Devinder Dhallu's one-sentence takeaway

You must always be marketing – especially if you can't afford a prime location.

DON HOLLY

Roaster and Barista Business Consultant

Don has been involved in coffee bars and roasting since the very beginning of the specialty coffee growth – building brands, researching trends, directing SCAA, discovering science, quality controlling at Green Mountain, communicating at every sensory level – and now consulting and advising a select group and still enjoying life to the full. One of the most experienced world coffee experts on the planet, we are so delighted to have his contribution.

What is the one thing you wish you'd known before you started?

Imagine having as your first mentor in the coffee business a man who was a multi-generational grower, manufacturer of his own coffee roaster, trained in roasting in Italy; someone who imported his own coffee via his Volkswagen van in a 6000-mile round-trip, and had already been retailing in Southern California for ten years before you met him. Such was my luck.

This man had more breadth of knowledge than just about anyone I have ever met since in the coffee industry: his name was Carl Diedrich. One of his sons, Stephen, took his father's coffee roasters design in the early 1980s and has turned that into one of the most successful coffee roaster manufacturing businesses in the world, selling more small-batch roasters than any other company. Stephen's older brother, Martin, was my business partner in opening up a dozen coffee houses in Orange County from 1984–94. That was really good fun, and to have that quality of coffee knowledge gave us a huge competitive advantage in the industry at that time.

So what is the one thing I wish I had known before I started? Mine's a very different answer than I think most folks getting into the coffee business would give. Their answer would be to have knowledge and mastery around coffee – how to cup, how to roast, how to brew – as that has huge competitive value. Given that we already had that at Diedrich Coffee, we were more focused on learning how to run the business and all of the challenges one faces in the financial, personnel and operational aspects that can make or break you. Fortunately, I had also been lucky in having excellent training and experience in business management before partnering with the Diedrichs, so that's what I brought to the party.

I wish we'd had back then what the current generation takes for granted. We didn't have Espresso Labs, Barista competitions, the Cup of Excellence, the Roaster's Guild. We had to learn much of the science and art of coffee the hard way, even though we had the heritage of the Diedrich family. It wasn't until I became the administrative director for the SCAA in 1995, when I learned how to use a TDS meter for measuring soluble solids, that I understood how to dial in a grinder to control extraction. It wasn't until David Schomer published *Barista Techniques* and his *Café Latte Art* videos that I learned how to make great espresso drinks. Our coffee houses were successful despite that, but I can imagine how much more successful they would have been if we'd had the knowledge that is fairly ubiquitous now.

What do you believe is the secret to success of your business and great coffee shops and cafés in general?

So, what was the secret of our success? Passion. We loved coffee and coffee houses. There is nothing in business that comes close to the amount of love you can have for a product and a place of operation than you can feel for coffee and coffee houses. I studied the history of coffee houses as we were building our fleet of stores, everything written I could find. I would travel across the country and to Europe and visit every coffee house and espresso bar I could find to found out about best practices and gain a deeper understanding. Everyone I met – and I was so fortunate to get to know so many wonderful people in our industry around the world – I tried to learn from, finding that there was never an end to the opportunity to share with fellow lovers of our product.

This passion for our industry is contagious. Your customers feel it. Your staff believes in it. Your community adopts you and considers you a part of the necessary fabric. Your business succeeds as a result of it.

True, there are at least a thousand other things you have to do right to be successful in the coffee business. Choosing great retail locations is important, because it is nearly impossible to make a profit unless you have a great location. Managing a great team well is critical, because it's the people you surround yourself with that make it work and worthwhile. But, even if you got those parts right, without passion I think you would be a failure.

Our business is truly remarkable. The more you understand coffee and coffee houses, the more you realize this. Devote yourself to it – mind, body and soul – and you will be living life with purpose and meaning.

HUGO – SIDE STORY

I first met Don at the 1998 annual conference of the Specialty Coffee Association of America in Denver. He was persuaded to come to Ireland to give us the benefit of his wisdom and I was asked to look after him and more or less act as his guide. This was very much from a geographical perspective, but what I learnt in those three days I have never forgotten. I tell Don Holly stories almost on a weekly basis – and I am absolutely serious about that.

That has to make Don probably the most influential coffee expert I have ever met. Certainly I have met many since that have had massive impact on me, but there was something about Don saying to us, 'Have you guys never torn up a grinder before?' and then proceeding to take some tools out of his bag and actually take two different grinders apart and put them back together again in thirty minutes – at the same time teaching us what to look for and what to do to make a better cup of coffee. Understanding the grind is one of the taste fundamentals, and I had only ever seen techs do it like that before as, obviously, I could dial in.

Don also said to me, having had me apologise for giving him a really bad coffee on Belfast's Lower Newtownards Road of an early morning, 'You have to understand that it's either the best or the worst cup of coffee you have ever tasted because you have nothing to compare it to.' A real sensuality lesson. The next morning in a Dublin Hotel, he pulled a grinder, a French press and whole bean Huila from his bag and made the best cup of coffee I had tasted in a long time, and at 6.30 a.m.

Of course he is also the master of the riposte and when asked on live Irish breakfast television if coffee was in his opinion better than sex, he replied, 'Not with my wife it's not'. We love Mrs Holly too!

Don Holly's one-sentence takeaway

Great passion is contagious and affects not just your staff but your customers too.

EDWARD BERRY

Ludlow Food Centre

Edward has a background career progression in a number of different areas – hotel management, wine, marketing, coffee, tea and cafés. He is now Managing Director at The Ludlow Food Centre. The centre employs its own artisan food makers to produce food for sale on-site, using both the estate's produce (livestock and dairy) and local growers to supply a butchery and produce ready meals and deli items. On top of this, the centre roasts its own espresso blend and single-origin coffees in an on-site coffee room. There are two cafés, one 140-seater on-site and a small outlet in Ludlow itself, and a fifteen-bedroom hotel with bar and restaurant.

www.ludlowfoodcentre.co.uk

What is the one thing you wish you'd known before you started?

In terms of interest to your readers, I will look at the two main café outlets. Whilst we serve coffee in the hotel, sales here are predominantly to guests staying overnight for breakfast service, and after meals. Therefore, the café/coffee elements are not the drivers.

Two years ago, we planned to take a sixty-seat café, with limited kitchen and call order service, and take it to 140 seats plus additional outside seating with table service and a full kitchen. We had good reason to undertake the project: the café was not able to cope with the numbers and limits on its function. However, although today I can report that it is a thriving, busy and profitable business, we had to go through a number of months of pain to get there.

Things that we needed to be aware of before we started:

- Regular customers find changes difficult, and as regular customers believe they have some sense of ownership. So, if you are going to do this sort of exercise, you could ask for input (you will never get consensus), but whatever you do, be prepared to lose some regulars simply because they don't like the changes in décor, menu, service etc.

- We did, however, listen to customers' food preferences and have worked out a menu to include these.

- Interestingly, whilst we lost some regulars, we now have a much larger group of regulars; numbers are up – as is average spend.

- If you plan to introduce table service, be aware of the much higher staff costs associated with this decision. You will have to get the average spend up and watch the dwell time if you are busy. You also need to be aware of lunchtime tea and cake consumption, as this will not help your spend.

- We opened a new outlet within the town. Its point is to sell and serve produce from the Ludlow Food Centre – in effect, a self-controlled wholesale outlet. Small towns in particular have their own issues – small population, limited takeaway trade compared to cities, seasonal business and quiet early weekdays. The absence of takeaway means that you need sufficient space for sitting in.

- While cities have driven the modern wave of coffee appreciation, in the sticks there's still a long way to go. So don't be surprised if your customers a) just ask for a white coffee, b) question the price, c) get confused by the offering, and d) complain that the coffee you serve is cold!

What do you believe is the secret to success of your business and great coffee shops and cafés in general?

It's a bit of a list:

- Get to know your customers
- The right staff
- Staff training
- Footfall/location
- Be aware of and do better than the competition
- Know your business. A busy café is, of course, not necessarily a profitable one.

We have built a following over several years and for many a visit to the Food Centre forms a regular part of their week. That being said, we are on a major road with other reasons to stop (shop, walk) and free parking, and we have plenty of impulse and seasonal business.

We also have a point of difference – we produce (breed, grow, cure, smoke, make, roast, bake, etc.) most of the food ourselves.

JOHNNY – SIDE STORY

Make no mistake, this is a multiple moving-part business. And as such, will never be easy to run. It makes my head spin to observe all that they do despite involvement in a chain of garden centres with cafés being a part of my own history.

But you can see from Edward's background that he has a lot of previous experience. These kinds of businesses are very much on the rise, where you mix a shopping experience with the ultimate outcome of providing a cup of coffee or the ingredients for an evening meal.

The key issue, like so many businesses of this type, is to ensure you have great people heading up each department or discipline. That way you can avoid the overwhelm that can often occur with so much going on.

HUGO – SIDE STORY

I know Edward because I am great friends with his partner Victoria Bishop, and my side story involves her because it highlights in my opinion such an important point in business.

Cutting a long story short, I helped Victoria at the start when they both were opening The Armadillo Café Ltd, and because I really liked her attitude we trained her in Belfast without agreeing any fees. She called, arranged sessions and we facilitated – and usually went for a delicious lunch on her in the Michelin-starred Shanks restaurant next door to our training centre (where Victoria held tutored wine tastings by the glass, much to the amazement of fellow diners and genius chef Robbie Millar, who is sadly no longer with us).

Anyway, on opening the café, Victoria gave me a cheque for what she thought amounted to a reasonable fee, saying that she thought that was at least what she owed me for our time. Amazing. I am pleased to say I didn't take it because she was so genuine (and thankfully, through her advice and help over the years, she has handsomely repaid us).

Being grateful for support from people and other businesses is such an essential lesson when starting and running businesses. And as Victoria demonstrated at a time she needed every penny to open her new business, gratitude with action is massively powerful even when it can be potentially painful.

Edward Berry's one-sentence takeaway
Make sure you have a point of difference – you must give the customer a strong and clear reason to visit you rather than the competition.

GARY MCGANN

Beyond the Bean

Gary is Sales and Marketing Director with Beyond the Bean, having effectively created the 'everything but the coffee' category in the UK and Ireland. Involved in the coffee business now for twenty years, he came from a hotel management background to create Espresso Warehouse with the late, brilliant David Williamson. Seriously experienced and network resourced, Gary is the 'go to man' for us all when we need something confirmed or validated.

www.beyondthebean.com

What you really should know before you open a café

Opening a café is like opening any other business – sounds obvious but often it's not. So many new people thinking about opening a café talk about their passion for coffee, but very little about their business model, financial structure, and business risk assessment of a financial nature.

When you have people over for dinner and cook a great meal you may get compliments that would persuade you to open a restaurant, but you may forget that these guests have drunk your wine and are your friends, so are inclined to say nice things. The proof in the pudding (pardon the pun) is to try your food in an environment where people have to pay for it and will either vote with their feet or give you honest feedback.

When planning your new café venture, get a clear sight of all your costs and split them into fixed and variable. The fixed you have little control over: rent, rates, refuse collection and to some degree an element of your utilities. What you can control are the variables – goods and staff costs being the two core ones.

When I worked in restaurants, we often modelled on three business levels when it came to staff – open with zero customers, open with 50 per cent capacity and open flat out at 100 per cent capacity. New market entrants often forget the first one – open with zero customers. At this level you still need some basic staffing, so there is also a fixed cost that applies to labour.

When and if you open, a key metric needs to be average transaction value – if most of your customers are only buying coffee, your gross margin may be great but your average transaction low, so in effect your contribution to your fixed overheads will be minimal. As the old saying goes, you cannot take a percentage to the bank. Work hard on your average transaction value by adding sales of incremental items to your core coffee offer that balance with your theme and values. The efficiency that this will bring to your business will greatly help your profitability.

Another key point is to factor your own labour costs into your model – if you were a city banker who was making lots of cash, you would not merely put a 20k salary for yourself into your calculations just to make the figures look good – you would only be kidding yourself.

In summary – model well financially, keep to your business principles in terms of offer that will differentiate you, and persevere; a new business needs at least six months to establish itself, but you must know when to admit failure. Throwing good money after bad is just foolish.

JOHNNY – SIDE STORY

Gary, being Gary, went slightly off-piste with his response but, if I'm honest, I encouraged him to do so. So why was Gary allowed this indulgence?

Put simply, I'll always listen to Gary because I almost never come away from a conversation where I haven't thought 'Ahhhhh – I hadn't quite thought of it that way.' Having set up nineteen different businesses over the last thirty years it's rare that I say that.

What Gary writes may seem like common sense, but it's worth reading more than once. His depth of experience and understanding of the industry – both as an operator and supplier – is huge. The first sentence of his last paragraph is one to put on your fridge door.

HUGO – SIDE STORY

All industries thrive on networking and Gary is a master. He is well connected because he adds so much value to people, and at the end of the day, as Jeffrey Gitomer says, 'All things being equal, people buy from people they like. All things not being equal, people still buy from people they like'!

Johnny sums Gary up very well, and from his early days selling coffee in Ireland for the late great David Williamson – where they both then created the coffee accessory category in the UK – to his many contributions to the industry, he is one of those people that we both say wholeheartedly 'knows his chops'.

Gary McGann's one-sentence takeaway

Know your average transaction value and work on this weekly with your team.

HUGO HERCOD

Relish, Cornwall

Raised an expatriate in the Far and Middle East, Hugo moved to the UK in his late teens. Whilst excelling at sport, he underwhelmed academically despite attending brilliant schools, so plumped for a degree in hotel and catering management at Portsmouth Polytechnic. After researching his dissertation on the revival of Britain's real ale micro brewers, he commenced his career as a *saisonnier* in the French Alps, interspersed with summers teaching windsurfing and sailing in the Mediterranean. Returning to the UK somewhat burnt out, he worked in hotels, pubs, restaurants and café's before redundancy gave him the impetus to open Relish Food & Drink in Wadebridge, Cornwall. In 2008 he won the UK Barista Championship, came tenth at the World Barista Championship and has since concentrated on establishing Relish as one of Cornwall's best cafés.

www.relishfoodanddrink.co.uk

What is the one thing you wish you'd known before you started?

I'm sorry, but it depends.

It depends on the day of the week, the time of year, how long it was since my last holiday, the last profound customer conversation, the most recent disaster, the bank balance . . . I could go on. If there's one constant in running a café, it's how wildly things can go from good to bad and back again – and hardly ever as a result of one thing.

Last year it was a £13,000 service charge bill from my landlord; I could have punched him.

Whilst I'm currently blessed with a great team, I wish I'd known how infuriating and exasperating employing my own staff could be. I had worked with plenty of poor staff in the past, but I hadn't necessarily chosen them and I wasn't giving them my own money at the end of the week. I am not much of a staff manager; I try to be a fair, kind and considerate but often my reward was being let down or taken advantage of.

I wish I'd known how much of my life was going to be consumed by my business and how I'd sometimes resent it. I managed pubs when I was young and at times I'd be expected to work a ninety-hour week; my last employer before Relish had me working forty days straight, without a day off. Having sworn to never let that happen again, we opened Relish six days a week, daytime only. That still required a sixty-hour week but then there was the ungodly amount of behind-the-scenes admin that nobody sees. It's taken several years to reach a happy balance, even though the solutions were there all along.

I wish I'd known how toxic a business partnership with a partner can be, especially when communication breaks down and all you've talked about for five years is the business. When everyone suggested a partnership agreement in case things go wrong, I wish I'd listened even though it felt like planning to fail. It has cost me dearly, though I'm not convinced any sort of agreement would have made it any less painful.

On a positive front, I wish I'd known how fulfilling owning my own business was going to be. I wish I'd done it earlier, hadn't been so cautious. I wish I'd backed myself and trusted my character and experience to get me through.

What do you believe is the secret to success of your business and great coffee shops or cafés in general?

I think it's about character. I know it may sound conceited or narcissistic and I'd hate to be thought of as anything like that, but I believe I am the right sort of person for the job.

I love eating and drinking, more than nearly anyone I know. A friend once told me that she loved to watch me eat because I always seemed to be enjoying it so much. I am equally delighted by a piece of perfectly ripe cheese, a glass of single malt whisky or a slice of good cake. I marvel at the skill of the makers, their mastery of the process, the dignity it gives them. I also love the history of it, how the best foods have evolved over generations, sometimes hundreds of years of thought, care, attention and knowledge, built on and rightly valued. I want to know about all of it because that makes the experience better, then I want to share it with like-minded people – my customers!

I am constantly curious. Having opted to take my degree in hotel and catering management for all the wrong reasons, I found myself in the hospitality and catering trade and I loved it. Wherever I travelled or worked I'd try and get a flavour of the region, the good, the bad, the indifferent. German perfection-ism, Californian service, Arabic hospitality, French professionalism. I'd have to be honest and say I haven't found much inspiration in England, excepting our ability to brew exceptional ales and brilliant cheeses. All my best memories are around food and drink and the people I've shared it with. My business draws on all of these experiences: it's my personal perfect café deli.

I think I'm a people person. I like to be liked and I want to be well thought of by others. This makes me happy to serve, keen to please, willing to go the extra mile to give a good impression. I hate to let customers down; I have nightmares about forgetting orders and ruining people's meals. Sometimes I think this is my biggest weakness.

I like working with my hands, crafting things like bread or, I suppose, cups of coffee. I'm lucky that most things come quite easily to me – I will make a good potter one day. Everything we can make at Relish we do, which makes it infinitely better than anything made in a factory. Customers really notice the difference.

I like spreadsheets, graphs, the complexity and breadth of the financial side of the job. I like to be challenged and I love to solve problems; the intellectual challenge of something so seemingly easy really satisfies me. This means that on the several occasions things could have gone financially tits up, they didn't.

Stubbornness and pride both help. There have been years when I should have given up, sold up and trained as a dentist. I was trying to earn a living and failing miserably; I clearly didn't have the necessary grasp of what I was doing. I've lost count of the days when all I wanted to do was turn my back and walk away. I fantasised about locking the café door, posting the keys back through the letterbox, hopping on my bike and peddling off around Europe. Every time I've gone home, drank a bottle of wine, slept on it, woken up and got on with it.

I'm also happy to be rubbish at things while I learn them. If my business could talk it would wholeheartedly agree with that one . . .

JOHNNY – SIDE STORY

I've a huge amount of time for Hugo – he's an obsessive foodie like me and we've discussed how our diaries from a very young age discuss very little other than food. Hugo's diary entry, at the age of five, for Wednesday 28 January reads: 'I love the smell of cheese'. To see the actual image of this diary and a longer interview with more insight from Hugo, sign up for the additional information at www.wakeupandsellbook.com.

When you visit Hugo's café and deli in Cornwall you might regard it as the classic 'perfect lifestyle' business, but his insight above shows another side. As you scratch the surface you see the familiar traits of attention to detail, a very firm grasp of the numbers, and the desire to make sure that business partnerships are strong and not destructive.

Hugo Hercod's one-sentence takeaway

Make sure you never lose the curiosity and wonder of great food and drinks.

JACK GROOT

JP's Coffee

In 1993, Jack Groot created his first business, a coffee bar in Holland, MI. In 2013, his coffee shop was awarded third place in America's Best Coffeehouse competition and in 2014 was honoured as one of the 10 Best Coffeehouses in America by *USA TODAY* Travel Destinations. In 2007, Groot created an industry training school to provide education, training systems and videos, and consulting for those in, and going into, the coffee industry.

Jack successfully sold all his business holdings to a large local company and assisted them with the transition in 2014. He describes himself as 'temporarily retired' and 'pondering future endeavours'.

www.jackgroot.com

What is the one thing you wish you'd known before you started?

A few weeks ago, John Richardson contacted me to ask if would I contribute to a new book they were publishing; they were looking for certain coffee industry folk to answer two questions.

First off, let me say I could write a book on each of these questions (John gave me 1000 words, so no worries). They are fabulous questions, and I look forward to reading other responses.

Now, let me tell you a quick story. The figure $168 is burned in my memory. Why $168? Because $168 was JP's gross revenue on day two. Why day two and not day one? Because day two sales were lower than day one. Why is this important? Because, I did not give up; that number symbolises to me the years of 'intestinal fortitude', or guts as many would call it.

JP's Coffee and Espresso Bar, or JP's as it was soon known as, was birthed from nothing. When I say *nothing*, I'm not talking about money . . . although I had little and borrowed lots. Not *nothing* in terms of knowledge – my degree is in food service management and I spent the better part of three years researching small business, coffee and retail. And not *nothing* in terms of support, as my wife believed in me and supported me 110 per cent during those early seventeen-hour days.

When I say *nothing*, I mean there was no coffee industry. In 1993, Starbucks had around 200 stores. There was no coffee industry to speak of, at least nothing I could research . . . even if the Internet had existed. I had to go it on my own, figure out the best I could how to make my dream a reality and not a nightmare. Why is this important to mention here? Because, although the world has been consuming coffee for centuries, the specialty coffee industry as it exists today, has really only existed for a few years. And that information is critical in framing my thoughts to John's questions.

Fast forward 20-plus years and JP's is by all accounts successful: thriving, busy, profitable and the recipient of national and even international recognition (JP's was recognised by *USA Today* as one of 'USA's Top 10 Coffeehouses' in February 2014). So successful that shortly after that recognition it was acquired by a larger local coffee roaster/retailer (yeah, go ahead and say it).

So, what *is* the one thing I wish I'd known back before November of '93? Well, it's not that I needed enough capital, as a lot of money might have screwed up my drive for efficiency. It's not latte art, as latte art didn't really exist. It's not location, location, location, although I did happen to choose a fabulous location (not by my genius, but simply by recognising that Starbucks liked corner location so I should think about that). And it certainly isn't creating a great floor plan, although knowing that would have saved me $150,000 in recreating my store six years after it opened.

The one thing I wish I'd known before I started is . . . drum roll please . . . nothing. Yes, nothing. It's the journey, my friend, that makes it. Now would I have made more money/made better lattes/served customers better had I known more? Probably. But the reality is the journey is what made me, what made JP's, the way it is. And that is worth knowing.

Now, if John forces me to tell you the one thing you need to know before opening your store, I will tell you this one thing – the buck stops with you. You must lead. You must be the one who sets the tone, creates the systems and knows your coffee. You must thrill the customer, build relationships and do the right thing. All the time. You must treat others as you want to be treated – and that means employees first. You must have integrity in everything you do. And you must work hard every day at the basics: serving great coffee, with a smile, in a great store, with clean bathrooms.

Seriously, I could go on and on, but I need to get to an even better question . . .

What do you believe is the secret to success of your business and great coffee shops and cafés in general?

OK, this one would not take up a whole book – it would take a whole series of books. This is the secret sauce, the key, the raison d'être of my existence. Are you ready for it? I love to serve others, or more accurately, to see them happy.

Another story – when I first opened JP's, I remember attractive, upper-class thirty- or forty-something women coming in ordering a latte, wondering if I could I make it 'skim milk, sugar free'. Well, my goal was not simply serving coffee – it was eliciting smiles* (oops, cat just exited bag, you've got some *secret sauce* on your chin). Once they ordered their coffee from the lowly bar boy (aka me) they went back to conversations about house, car and hubbie. But alas, I was not done.

'*How would you like a piece of Chocolate Diva?*' (JP's fabulous chocolate torte), I'd say.

'*Oh no, I can't have that!*' they'd reprove me.

'*Ahh, I see, well how about a piece of our baklava cheesecake? You know, my wife used this recipe to take first place in a local recipe contest. Matter of fact, it beat every competing recipe from every category.*'

'*Sorry, I can't. That would be bad,*' was a common response from the slightly uptight, definitely well-maintained women who frequented our upscale downtown.

But, then it would happen. Somewhere in the conversation, as I smiled with a wee glint in my eye and got them to look at me, they would see I was less interested in selling them something and more interested in simply brightening their day, having fun, maybe even teasing them a bit. Then it happened – they smiled back.

I win. Game over. Success. 'This' is easy.

'This' isn't about selling coffee, although it is. 'This' isn't about great baked goods, but it is. 'This' isn't even about being a great third place, although it is. 'This' is about eliciting smiles. Making people happy. You see if you are more concerned with making people happy and less concerned about making money, you will make money. Interesting conundrum, I know. There is something that happens when you make people happy . . . they tell other people about the place that made them happy (hint: and has great coffee, clean bathrooms, etc.).

Wow, a thousand words already.

OK, my final words . . . the three main reasons I agreed to write this article:

1. In some small way I hope it encourages and enlightens you, the reader.
2. I hope someday to be interviewed by John, simply to enjoy his Irish accent.
3. My seven degrees of separation from Gordon Ramsay will be reduced to one.

JOHNNY – SIDE STORY

I've been familiar with Jack for many years but before now had very little contact with him. In many ways he does very similar work to what Hugh and I do but in the US. He's very active in various groups online (especially LinkedIn) and I'm always impressed by how much common sense he talks. Unlike many of the advisors that exist on both sides of the Atlantic, he has a lifetime of real world experience and I've never read anything he's written and not thought, 'I'm not sure I could have put that any better!'

Jack Groot's one-sentence takeaway

Responsibility: 'the buck stops with you' – still the biggest lesson that owners and managers need to grasp . . . and often don't.

JAMES SHAPLAND

ex Coffee #1

James is an ex-investment banker who built a fifteen-strong chain of stores in South Wales and the South West called Coffee #1. In 2011, he sold the business to a large independent brewery company. This was, in our opinion, the most profitable and focused exit from the business that we've seen.

What is the one thing you wish you'd known before you started?

There are 307 variables that contribute to making a cup of coffee good, and more than 503 to making a cup of coffee great. Starting with the origin, the quality of harvest, the roaster, the roast profile, the blend, the grinder, the espresso machine, the water, the milk, the extraction, the pour etc.

Under each heading, there are about two dozen component parts which must work in sync to ensure a quality outcome. We developed a flow chart delineating the perfect sequence. We showed 'what if' scenarios should the process break down at any stage.

When I started, I thought it would be easy to churn out top quality coffee quickly. I went in with a blasé attitude. The result was a poor quality experience for our customers and a failed business model.

What do you believe is the secret to success of your business and great coffee shops and cafés in general?

Open-book management. The value of transparency cannot be overstated. Generally, if you don't educate your people about the business, they will assume you make far more money than you actually do. And when that happens you generally lose far more money than you should. In fact, in the early stages of development it is not uncommon for employees to make more money than the owner himself. Through *The Great Game of Business* by Jack Stack we discovered a new way to educate employees, enhance their development and drive profits substantially higher. We would sit down with managers and ensure they understood all key metrics within the P&L. It sounds a little stale. But when you turn it into a game and managers understand the role they play, they become small business owners. This leads to higher levels of engagement.

Becoming obsessive compulsive. Constantly analyse competition within the sector and across the global hospitality/retail scene. Wherever I went, I was constantly switched on to the idea of continuous improvement. I carried a notebook everywhere and noted down places where the experience was out of the ordinary. I remember watching the Virgin in-flight safety video and thinking it was a revelation in terms of creativity and lateral thinking. Similar admiration was felt for Intelligentsia Coffee – such courage to push the boundaries so far outside the norm.

Education, education, education. I went to the Coffee Fest trade shows in New Orleans, Anaheim and Seattle. I went to visit coffee plantations in Costa Rica and India. I learnt how to 'cup coffee' with the leading roasters in the UK. I encouraged staff to compete in UK Barista Championship. I attended Cranfield University's business growth programme. I even brought in John Richardson to help us as we grew! No stone was left unturned in my desire to develop all the angles involved in enhancing the customer experience.

Share the wealth. Prepare the top team for the journey well in advance and ensure they can see the pot of gold at the end of the rainbow. Howard Schulz once described the UK coffee scene as the most competitive market anywhere in the world. In order to succeed as a small business against the powerhouses of Nero, Starbucks and Costa you need to turn the ordinary into extraordinary. To do this you need senior staff and core players to go above and beyond. To feel incentivised to do this they need to have some grasp of the exit-strategy concept and how their immense contribution will pay dividends.

Admit that you're a bit of a plonker in many aspects of the business. Get out of your own way and bring in the specialists to clear up your mess. Jack of all trades and master of none is something for which I anticipate recognition in the New Years' Honours List. It is very easy to try and cover all bases and never quite get any of them right. Because you are watching the pennies, you will sometimes avoid paying top dollar for specialist advisors or the best employees. This is a huge mistake, leading to burn-out and losses. To succeed you must identify individuals with a unique set of skills. And then try to let them flourish. It is hard to let go, but you will create a stronger, more successful business in the long run.

David v Goliath. Revel in the fact that you are a small business with the room to innovate and change up the category as and when the need presents itself. When I decided to open two shops either side of Starbucks in Roath, Cardiff, my dad came to me and asked for a quiet word in my ear. 'Well you're off your f**kin' 'ead you are . . . you been sniffin' glue you silly sod?' Three months later we opened the second store and . . . it took off. Twelve months later, Starbucks, who had been first on the scene in Roath, put up the To Let boards. They were heading out! This was the most satisfying moment of the journey. Throughout my father's ear bashing I was adamant that we provided a far better experience for a £2 cup of coffee. It was as simple as that. Didn't matter who they were. I believed our customers had a far richer, warmer experience and so we were right to expand.

JOHNNY – SIDE STORY

There's a book in the story of Coffee #1 (and it may well happen), but even in these few words there is a tremendous amount to learn from James. I was lucky enough to travel much of this journey with James and learnt as much from him as he did from me.

We see a lot of people coming into the industry who seem convinced there is a lot of easy money to be made. As you'll have learnt yourself, read from our books or gathered from the other interviewees – this is simply not the case. This is why we emphasise the passion part of our model so strongly. If you open up and expect to make millions, then you are hugely misguided and headed for a painful and humiliating fall.

That is not what James did though – despite his city background. When I first started working with him, he had seven sites already operational and a very clear financial plan and outcome in place. But, and it's a big but, this was all secondary to his desire to create a business that provided substantially better service and quantifiably better coffee all wrapped up in an appreciably cleaner environment than the big chains were producing.

I think his story about Starbucks gives you a decent measure of just how effective he was at seeing through those targets.

From my perspective James was both a joy to deal with and also very tough. His focus was immense and he literally applied, in a tested and controlled manner, everything that I suggested. One example of this is that he took our first book and had a full-time member of staff working to ensure that all its fifty-two tips were implemented into the business.

It was at Coffee #1, and through working with James, that I learnt about the value of observing, in micro detail, customer behaviour through the business. On several occasions we attempted to analyse and discover the 'secret sauce' of his most successful store. That involved video recording a day's full service and watching every customer from the front door to the coffee delivery area.

To attempt to come up with meaningful conclusions I then had to sit down and edit down into smaller chunks hours and hours of video. This may sound like hell but it was actually one of the most useful exercises I've ever undertaken, and those days of editing have shaped every aspect of the staff and manager training that I've created or undertaken since.

With the bonus material at www.wakeupandsellbook.com you can find a much longer interview with James and I strongly advise that you check it out.

James Shapland's one-sentence takeaway

There are more than 503 ways of making a cup of coffee great – imagine if you applied that level of detail to every aspect of your business?

JO HAMILTON-WELSMAN

Coffee #1

Jo is the Operations Manager of Coffee #1. She worked with James Shapland until his successful sale of the business and has continued to help develop the business to the fifty-plus sites that exist today. Her skills as an operations manager are as good as we've ever seen.

www.coffee1.co.uk

What is the one thing you wish you'd known before you started?

To be honest, the things I wish I had known before I started would have probably put me off working in hospitality as it is such bloody hard work. Had I known about the challenges and difficulties beforehand I probably wouldn't be where I am today.

What do you believe is the secret to success of your business and great coffee shops and cafés in general?

First and foremost there must be a shared passion. In order to succeed you must attract like-minded people into your business.

James [Shapland] and I worked well together because he had recognised my skill set and qualities and he was very willing to listen to my ideas and suggestions. He was passionate about his business and recognised that an operator like me who knew how to manage people well and train and develop a tcam would drive the business in the direction that he wanted. I wholeheartedly bought into the simplicity of the Coffee #1 ethos and vision and caught the 'BUG'!

To be honest, no business can be a success if you do not have the right people to help you achieve what you want. It is impossible to do it all yourself, and building a team of people that you can trust to drive your business alongside you is imperative.

I recall James talking to me about being a HERO (fire fighter), a MEDDLER (controller) and a STRATEGIST (working on the business, not in it). Everyone starts off as the HERO, and at the start you need to do lots of fire fighting. This is particularly apparent when there is a lack of systems and process, a lack of training and development, and a lack of talented people.

Inspiring, motivating, training and managing your people well is a worthwhile investment. It's bloody hard work, nothing ever seems good enough, you can't always please everyone, and no matter how hard you try someone always manages to make you feel as though you didn't try at all. If I can offer one bit of advice, it would be: 'Never give up!'

In the early days, James and I recognised that recruiting the wrong people into the business was damaging. Managers weren't trained to interview and they were looking for anyone willing to clear tables and wash dishes. Just bringing in an extra pair of hands was the immediate relief for a manager. We quickly took control and I became a 'meddler'. I recruited everyone in the business to ensure we got the 'right' people and worked towards creating a talented pool of people.

This proved to be one of the best decisions, and to this day, only those fully trained to recruit for Coffee #1 are able to employ anyone. You need to understand the profile of the people you want in your business and stick to it. Never compromise on your recruitment. Put time and effort into the pre-screening and interviewing process and follow a robust induction training process.

In Coffee #1 we have identified our best performing people, profiled their qualities and now ensure that these are the qualities we look for every time we interview. I look for like-minded, genuine, smiley, friendly, proud people pleasers.

An ambition to create an infectious energy and enthusiasm within our teams to drive the pride and passion that James instilled in me is paramount. You must be able to thrive on the pressures and demands that hospitality brings. It is a relentless business that challenges and tests your patience every day.

You will undoubtedly benefit from investing in training your people. There are many examples of how Coffee #1 has reaped the rewards of training. Ensure it is fun, engaging and interesting. People are motivated by being trained and your people pleasers will want to put their new skills into practise.

During the aggressive growth phase of Coffee #1 I had a simple ambition: to maintain the standards (3Cs – Coffee, Customer, Cleanliness) that James set at the outset. Having an eye for detail and never compromising on standards are imperative to the success of a business. I have a fastidious, consistent approach that everyone understands and no matter how many stores I have, my expectations remain the same.

What once seemed impossible to achieve, has now been

achieved. It just goes to show that if you put your mind to it and are determined not to compromise on standards, and continue to strive to be the best, you can do it.

It all comes back to robust systems and processes, identifying gaps, learning from mistakes and a willingness and desire to be the best.

I follow these basic rules to keep me on track as the business grows:

- Never turn a blind eye – EVER!
- Keep it simple
- Where there's a problem, there's a solution.

You need a fastidious approach to maintaining your standards, a determination to never give up and to be prepared to repeat yourself over and over again. Share your vision, refresh your teams and recognise areas for improvement – and ACT!

You have to be able to recognise your mistakes and never be afraid to admit to them, learn from them, apologise where necessary and make the necessary changes to prevent making the same mistake again.

Recognise that you can always learn from others. Listen to feedback and don't think that you are the one that should have all the answers. Most of the best ideas and suggestions I have implemented have come from others within the business.

Understanding what makes people tick is also very useful in getting the best out of your teams. Put time into understanding people. Not just your people but your customers too.

Set KPIs (Key Performance Indicators) against areas of business improvements. You can measure the success of your business by measuring the elements of the business that require improving.

Outline what improvements you want to make, for example smiling at the till, speed of service, table clearing, merchandising or financial performance.

- Is there a training gap?
- Is there a system/process in place?
- When you have trained the process and provided the tools to do it, measure it!

Ensure you have robust systems and processes for all elements of your business. Keep it simple, though. For example, you don't need to have expensive programmes to know whether your business is profitable. Just ensure you are optimising and identifying opportunities for improvement.

Drive sales – learn how to do this, set targets and create a culture of record breaking.

Margin control – manage this daily through effective delivery receipts; chase credits, control portions, manage wastage and count your stock!

Wage control – too low is compromising on service, too high is compromising on service!

Contribution – manage your business like your home! Save energy, look after your equipment, have a budget for disposable/consumable costs.

JOHNNY – SIDE STORY

I've a tremendous amount of time and respect for Jo. I worked hand in hand with her on multiple training initiatives and she was a pleasure to be around. Endlessly dedicated, hardworking and incredibly efficient – all the usual things you might expect me to say about an operations manager who grew a business from two or three sites to fifty.

But . . . Jo had a little bit of magic in her too. She was able to demonstrate to me, in the most graphic way possible, just how important a good manager can be. It was a demonstration that I'd never seen before.

There's some proper gold dust in her answers; when Jo says 'drive sales' in her bullet points it may sound like common sense or a trite line from a business book, but in reality how she achieved this was quite remarkable. For a multi-site manager at any level there is always a balance between working hands-on at various sites and making sure you are 'working on the business' and developing the rest of the team.

Jo's skill as a 'hands-on' manager, when carefully orchestrated, was extraordinary. If for example, a manager was going to be absent from a certain site on a Saturday, Jo would announce that she'd be along to manage – and that they were going to break the sales record. When I first heard this I thought it was bravado, but on my next visit I would discover that that is exactly what they did.

When I asked how she did it (because I, like the rest of the planet, am looking for immediate gratification and one simple solution I discovered that it was basically all about raising expectations and energy. It was a simple (or not so simple) process of applying much of what she talks about above. Sure, they would take samples out to the street if sales slowed, but in general it was all about driving the staff to create a vibrant and fun atmosphere and then the customers would inevitably come along for the ride.

Jo Hamilton-Welsman's one-sentence takeaway

Systematically build a recruitment and induction process to ensure you have real energy within your shop.

PASCAL WRENN

Pascal Coffee House

Pascal runs Pascal Coffee House in Galway. You'll find more details on their Facebook page.

(Rather than starting with a basic introduction, Pascal has a longer story that I thought would be useful to tell. If you can ignore the obvious praise towards me and Hugh that is inherent within the telling of it (he loves our books), you will find some important lessons for those of you who may be thinking about franchises.)

First of all, let me say a big thank you to you and Hugh for your book *Wake up and Smell The Profit*. It, along with others, saved my business and I'd like to tell you, briefly if I can, my story:

I am thirty-four years old, have been in the catering industry most of my working life, originally in the UK, then in Galway, Ireland where I moved in 2005 to be with my now wife, Aine.

My dream had always been to own and run a coffee shop. When I arrived in Ireland, I got myself a job as store manager with a small coffee shop chain as a way of learning the ropes. It was a great company, with vision and really good people at the wheel. At the time it had around seven or eight stores in Galway and Dublin, some franchised and some company owned. After a couple of years, the opportunity came along for me to open up my own franchised store in a place called Moycullen, a little town outside Galway City.

It all made sense, the business plan was sound and the location was great. After spending nearly €200k on fit-out, equipment and franchise fees, I was ready. It was March 2008 when I opened the door . . .

. . . A week before the Lehman Brothers' bank went bust. To say it all went downhill from there would be an understatement. However, I put my trust in my franchisor, hoping that they would guide me through it, but that help never came. The good people that actually knew how to run the company had been let go, and the support the franchisees were getting was pretty much non-existent.

I stuck it out for three years, somehow managing not to lose any money but not getting anything out of it for myself. I learned VERY quickly how to control my costs, and became very good at it. In April 2011, the opportunity to move location came up. So I did, thanks to a reasonable landlord letting me out my fifteen-year lease with no consequences.

The new location was exciting, the next best thing to being on the Galway City High Street, just a few steps off it. I negotiated good lease terms and packed my bags – tables, chairs, picture frames, spoons, forks etc. – and relocated. The unit had actually previously been a coffee shop so refurbishment was minimum. By that time, I was one of only two franchises remaining; the others had unfortunately succumbed to the recession, a recession that, by the way, here in Ireland was horrendous.

So on to the second chapter, still under the same franchised name, motoring along waiting for the tide to turn . . . but it didn't. Now being in a city-centre location, my sales were much higher, but so were my overheads. I soon came to realise that the great name I signed up to in 2008 wasn't so great any more – the customers got bored, the menu never changed of course, as the company had got rid of their head chef. So came the biggest and best decision of my business life: drop the franchise and DO MY OWN THING!!

I was nervous, but I started to do my research, and read a lot, and this is how I came across *Wake Up and Smell the Profit* and *The E-Myth Revisited* by Michael Gerber. I simply could not stop reading those two books. They made so much sense. I was already on the same wavelength and reading them just proved I wasn't crazy.

So in April 2013, after telling (not asking) my franchiser I was getting out of my ten-year agreement with him, I refurbished and re-branded to Pascal Coffee House – my wife came up with that – because who likes the sound of their own name – but it works. Thanks to my chef background, I created a new menu. I also came up with systems and procedures – from which direction the tables should be wiped to which way the handled cups should be facing on top of the coffee machine. I realised the importance of treating staff well and discovered how important they are and to treat them with the respect they are worth (happy staff = happy customers). And I discovered the benefits of working 'on the business' more than 'in it'.

IT PAID OFF. It is now March 2015; I have pretty much doubled my sales since leaving the franchise to €500k and I'm finally making real money. We are rated the number-one café in Galway on TripAdvisor and number four out of 355 restaurants! And we're not even a restaurant but a coffee shop. We do breakfast and sandwiches . . . but they are by far the best breakfasts and sandwiches you will find here in Galway. I am currently on the lookout for premises to expand to a second Pascal Coffee House!

What is the one thing you wished you'd known before you started?

My answer is that I wish I'd come across your book!

What I've learned in the last couple of years is to trust your gut instinct and don't doubt yourself – and your book helped me with that.

What, in your opinion, is the secret to success of your business and great coffee shops and cafés in general?

Your staff are the most important part of your business (even more so than your customers)

Without a great team behind you, the customers will simply not be there. When I place an ad for new staff, I mention as essential a great personality and sense of humour. When I get someone in for a trial shift I look for the following qualities in this order:

1. Personality
2. Sense of humour
3. Common sense
4. Experience

You can train someone with a good personality and plenty of common sense to gain the experience you're looking for, but NEVER the other way around.

I treat my staff with the same respect I expect from them. I never ask anyone to do anything I wouldn't happily do myself.

Friendly, helpful staff are mentioned in nearly every single one of the reviews we get. You can only achieve this if your staff are happy working in your coffee shop. They have to *want* to be there and care about the business nearly as much as you do.

Systems and procedures

This is something that I've always believed in, but every time I mentioned it to various business people I knew, they looked at me as though I was mad or had some sort of OCD disorder.

It wasn't until I read the two books I mentioned above that I realised I'd been right all along. And even more so, was amazed by the amount of businesses – especially pre-recession – that simply didn't care about systems and procedures. After all, why did they have to, during the Irish 'Celtic Tiger' it seemed you could open any kind of business with little to no experience and you'd be raking it in. I suppose those are the very businesses that didn't survive.

For the first few years, everything was stored in my head, I was there 24/7 and could deal with any problems on the spot. For the last two years, I have taken it all out of my head, and put it on paper – our operations manual. I found that the golden rule is to assume everyone is dumb (don't quote me on that!), every single little thing has to have a system or it just won't be done properly. We have regular staff meetings, and anything that's not working properly, or could be done better, is noted, and a new system put in place. We basically have an idiot-proof instruction manual for everything, from customer service to cleaning schedules etc . . .

We have daily checklists, comparable to an airliner's cockpit. They alone have lifted an enormous weight off my shoulders. I can come and go as I please without having to remind him or her to do this or that. I just know it will be done.

We pride ourselves on the fact that no matter how busy or quiet it gets, the customer will get the exact same level of service. If we feel sometimes it gets too busy, and that the level of service might drop, we simply don't let them in, and politely ask them to come back at a quieter time.

Here's a good example of how a simple system can make your life so much easier.

My bookkeeper would chase me every month for this or that credit card receipt. I would always misplace them, and it would take me a couple of hours and headaches to find and send them all on to her.

I now have a scanning app on my iPhone linked to a Dropbox folder at work, which my manager will print up once a week (one of the checklist items) and put in the relevant file, which ends up in my bookkeeper's hands at the end of the month. So if I'm out getting diesel, I get back in the car, scan the receipt with my phone, and that's it; I never have to worry or even think about it again.

Know your numbers

Numbers have always been my strong point; right from the start, I knew every cent that was going in and out and on what date. I could predict pretty accurately what my bank balance would be six months down the line. I have a cash-flow spread-sheet that I call my life-support machine – as it probably saved me from going under in the first three years of business. It is updated every month. LOOK AFTER YOUR CASH FLOW, AND YOUR P&L WILL LOOK AFTER ITSELF. It amazes me the amount of businesses that have no idea what is going in and out, and are constantly worried about what's to come. *If you know what's coming, good or bad, you don't get that worrying knot in your stomach.*

I could go on for ever, but you get the idea.

All in all, get your systems and procedures on paper, no matter how small your business is, and make it your operations manual. Ask yourself whether each system you have in place would work just as well if you weren't there or if you had another five shops. Know your numbers and keep a constant eye on your cash flow.

Most important of all, respect your staff and they will respect you and your business. Think of a personality you would like your business to be, and employ only people who fit in with that personality.

I'm not naive, I may be cocky now as my business is on the up, but every business has its ups and downs, and another down will come at some point. I am just going to make damn sure I'm ready for it.

JOHNNY – SIDE STORY

There are several key points to learn from Pascal's story. Firstly, it's important to be aware of how brutally hit Ireland was after the banking collapse. Ireland, both North and South, redefined the economic concept of a bubble. Many houses in Dublin and Belfast outstripped London prices, so when the bubble burst it was like a bomb going off (thankfully that's an unfortunate habit that we've also got over).

Ireland is still very much on its knees economically and so Pascal's story has to be taken within the context of that.

The message about franchises is very important. Some of them are, quite frankly, dreadful. Over the years Hugh and I have seen talented, hardworking and honest people bankrupted or nearly bankrupted by poor franchises. So if you are considering a franchise please, please do your homework and do NOT be taken in by the promise of great support and easy money.

Secondly, Pascal was lucky with his lease. Very often it can be a long lease that will bankrupt you if you make a mistake – always try to negotiate a break clause within the first three (or maximum five) years to avoid these issues. This will be easy or difficult to do depending upon the location and the state of the economy.

And finally, Pascal is obsessed with systems and processes. Every owner of a great coffee shop or business nearly always is. Read *The E-myth*.

Pascal Wrenn's one-sentence takeaway

Recruit great, focused people and train them in the necessary technical skills – not the other way round. It's almost impossible to train bad staff to be friendly and good with the customer.

PAUL RANKIN

Rankin Selection

Paul Rankin changed food the food landscape in Northern Ireland – at every level. In 1989, at a time when the troubles were still very much in evidence, he opened Roscoff in Belfast. This became the first restaurant in Northern Ireland to win a Michelin Star. He was responsible for training many of the best chefs throughout the 1990s and was a regular on many of the nation's TV food shows that developed during this era. At the height of his business he operated four restaurants, twelve cafés and a bakery. He now focuses on TV and brand consultancy work and the development and promotion of his range of Irish-based products.

www.rankinselection.com

What is the one thing you wish you'd known before you started?

I was well trained, skilful and passionate when I came back to Northern Ireland, and in the early days some great media work came my way that helped me enormously. But quite often, when somebody has a high profile, the money men can blow smoke up your ass and tell you that you can make a fortune . . . so we made a foray into expansion with the cafés and bakery.

My vision in those days was to have an equivalent of a Michelin-starred café where everything was handmade. We even made the bread that we used for our artisan sandwiches. It was unique and in my travels, I had never seen a café like that. So we baked everything ourselves, made all the food, and initially it was a roaring success.

It was, however, a very expensive operation to run and we incurred significant additional costs and expenses as a result of our expectation of high quality. That's probably the one thing that I would do differently if I was to go there again – charge more for it. Of course we had to understand that we were in Belfast, a significant factor with pricing. It was crucial to be competitive but we had a unique selling proposition that was hard to beat and so if we had charged more, we could have remained true to the original vision.

What I learnt that was so important was that you have to understand business and what people perceive your brand to be. Consumer perception is all that really matters, and properly understanding that takes a significant degree of effort to listen to what they say and to qualify it properly, because there are so many opinions. We made a few mistakes.

I think I was naive in this vision in that firstly I didn't think what the competitors were doing was good enough. They were all selling the same thing and our offer was so much better, but I didn't think about what the quality would look like when we got to ten or twenty sites. I should have looked carefully at that – at what was achievable. In reality, I realised that the bigger we got the more I was letting my customer, who was so impressed with our offer, down. Looking back on it, I really wish I could have looked at what we should have been doing to build the business, keeping consistency, and how I could deliver different products of a certain quality, unique to my ideas, that were not easy to copy.

I knew I was creative and had the ability to look at something and make it appetising. I was always able to have people say, 'That's delicious'! What is equally important, from a business point of view, is to understand where you are going to get the skill to execute that. We are always fighting a skills shortage. Maybe I should have gone to Spain or France, found the talent, figured out the answer and then how to 'freeze it' and bring it back. Ultimately, this was my responsibility and was one of the things I would focus more on now if I was back there.

What, in your opinion, is the secret to success of your business and great coffee shops and cafés in general?

In a way, you know it is great to be an idealist, but business is a hard mistress and will beat it out of you. It's really important to dare to dream, to have ideas, to have belief that you can make a difference, but you also need to take a cold hard look at how to achieve consistency, and the product you deliver must match the brand.

The other thing I would say looking back is that I wouldn't have flown quite as close to the wind from a risk point of view. You will make mistakes and you need to have the financial space to do that, recover and learn from it. We should have built in some consolidation space and I would say it's really important to have that safety net.

I am now doing TV and branding work. The Rankin Selection is going well – people see it as a relationship that they understand. Irish chef, Irish soda bread, Irish sausages . . . The customer says 'It makes sense' and I understand that. That's why it works. It has to make sense.

HUGO – SIDE STORY

I met Paul in a retail clothing changing room in East Belfast to discuss a potential coffee solution that was way ahead of its time. This guy wanted his own blend, and moreover he thought that it was important to have a 20 per cent Indonesian component because he wanted it full-bodied. He was only to end up one of Ireland's top chefs. What I learnt here was that any cuisine was all about recipe, detail and attention and that coffee was no different. It was 1989.

We went on to look after Paul's coffee requirements for many years with a sense of loyalty and care for what he was doing and awareness of the impact he made on a market that many underestimated.

Paul Rankin is a leader who had an amazing impact on the Northern Irish landscape. With his friendly banter, challenging questions and ability to really listen to what you had to say, he was one of those professionals that simply via a presence and positioning taught you to never bullshit and always admit when you didn't know something. He respected that. And we then had to find the answers, which grew our business because we had to go and learn.

Paul Rankin's one-sentence takeaway

Dare to dream but make sure you have very strict systems and processes in place to ensure that dream is consistently delivered.

PETER DORE-SMITH

Kaffeine

Peter is the owner of Kaffeine, based at Fitzrovia in London. He has recently opened his second café in the area, in Eastcastle Street. Peter's aim is to be always regarded as one of the leading cafés in the UK, but in reality Kaffeine is famous worldwide. Some of his recent awards include:

- Best Independent Café Europe – 2010
- Gold Award – Best Independent Sandwich Bar UK – 2011, 2014
- Gold Award – Best Independent Café UK – 2011, 2012, 2013, 2014
- TripAdvisor– Certificate of Excellence – 2012, 2013, 2014

http://kaffeine.co.uk

What is the one thing you wish you'd known before you started?

I think I am fortunate, or perhaps different to a few others in the café industry, in that I had twenty-five years of experience in front-of-house service and operations before Kaffeine. This of course prepared me for most things that have happened before, during and after opening the business, from the all-important finances, through recruitment and management of staff, to operations, customer service, food-safety management and procedures, food costs, operational efficiencies and details, cleanliness and professionalism.

There was one thing I was not prepared for though: the stress of opening. Opening and operating the business for the first six months was easily the hardest, most stressful, most challenging, most tiring thing ever to do. Proper hard. My wife was also pregnant with our first child, Layla, at the time and she was born six months after we opened. So it all happened in that first six months. I still have my cash-flow spreadsheet from that time and I can see that we had £1500 in the bank when she was born.

I used to suffer fom stress sickness and lost five kilos in weight, from 90 down to 85. We did not open on Sundays to start with, but I would wake up at 6 a.m. anyway, have breakfast, then go back to sleep on the couch for three hours, or go out for lunch and fall asleep at the table. So tired . . . so, so, so tired.

I remember taking the bus in to work at 5.30 a.m. most mornings, so I was able to help in the kitchen or get work done before starting on the floor for service, and looking at all the other businesses along the high street, taking inspiration from them and thinking if they can do it, then surely I can.

We have also just opened our second business and that is also very stressful, but not as hard as the first one; I never want to go through that again. However, it should be: it is a very serious thing, opening a business, a food business, where it is your job to employ people, look after them, make food and coffee, serve people, make sure you do not kill them with your food, or turn them away with your lack of service – and with a lot of investment and the potential to make, or lose, a lot of money. So it should be stressful; you need experience, courage and, as one man said to me once, 'very big balls'.

Of course we are where we are now, so obviously I made it through. They say that which does not kill you makes you stronger and it definitely did that. Nothing much fazes me these days. Of course I am still stressed and do not sleep, or wake up at 3 a.m., and I have a receding hair line, but when a problem comes around, it is more a case of 'OK, let's get it fixed then', and it is dealt with properly and effectively with minimum stress.

In the end, after opening my own business, just after the recession and having our first child six months later, plus everything else that has gone on since, it has made me much stronger and calmer, not just in business but with my family too.

There is one other thing I wish I'd known before opening . . .

This is quite simple – check the sewers. Get them cleaned, get them jetted, get a survey done. Invest the money. After that, understand how your sewers work and make sure you keep them maintained and clean.

At our original store, we've had all sorts of problems passed on from the previous tenant. I won't go into details, but anyone reading this who has worked for us in the past will probably know what I mean. It is a very, very unpleasant and costly problem.

The last thing you want, in the middle of service, when everything is going well and you're thinking, 'This is amazing, this is what it is all about!' is for your sewers to back up and overspill onto your floor, especially if it is pouring rain – then you are in serious trouble.

Even if you are operating now, and have never had this done, I highly recommend it as an insurance policy for the future.

And also that you make sure your kitchen team do not 'abuse' the pipes by putting grease and fat down them. A very safe measure is to once a week, check the flow of the water. We flush our toilets weekly and listen at the manholes for running water, so we know it is OK. I have my own sewer rods and heavy-duty gloves to be able to fix problems myself, as often it is easy to fix. We also have them cleaned annually, plus we put hot soapy water down once a month just to be sure.

For our new store, we had the drains all cleaned beforehand as a part of the lease negotiations at the landlord's expense. He was quite happy with this in the end actually, as it identified a problem further down his sewer line that needed to be addressed. This was fixed before we even started renovations work.

The other useful thing to know before you start up is how to save money by fixing things yourself. It can be as simple as changing a fuse, or knowing what to do if the water or the power goes off, or your till system fails. On top of this, make sure your key managers know how to fix these things, too. A simple thing like electricity can so often be taken for granted, but there is nothing worse than turning away customers because you have no power and do not know how to sort it out yourself.

What do you believe is the secret to success of your business and great coffee shops and cafés in general?

There is no one secret; if there was, it might be easier to open and run a coffee shop, or indeed any business. There are in fact many secrets, and the success of your business is dependent on how well you execute or achieve those secrets.

Qualified and relevant experience – nothing can beat this. An operator with twenty-five years' experience in the industry, against someone with none, will always have an advantage. This is obvious.

Planning – failing to plan, means planning to fail – An age-old saying, but one that is so true. When opening a business, or building one, it is critical to plan, plan, plan and plan again. It is also important to review those plans on a regular basis, to look back at what you have or have not achieved and to re-plan continuously.

Business is the art of war – Being in business is basically being in a hard-fought competition or a war, a very hard, long drawn-out one, with some fantastic results possible, or some huge failures. In order to go into competition like this, or into a war as such, you need to be prepared (see above) and to have:

- the right equipment
- the right leadership
- the right experience (see above)
- very good and deep funding
- support at home and in your family life
- the right team or army to support your vision, who believe in you and will do anything for you.

You also need to be fair, ruthless, able to listen, to act, to discipline, to promote, to train, to encourage, to support, to give opportunities, to provide – and to remove when necessary those who do not believe in your vision, or follow your rules and procedures.

You are now the general, the leader, the commander of your own little army, if you want to call it that, who will follow you into the trenches. But you need to be able to lead them and encourage them to do so.

Hospitality – this is the hospitality business – You are serving coffee, food, perhaps other beverages, even offering accommodation, but overall what you must be providing is genuine and friendly hospitality to your customers. This comes from the top and must filter down into all your procedures, structures and training. If you do not provide this simple ethic of being hospitable, then you are in the wrong industry.

Business: you are now in business – Being in business means being good at numbers and loving the back-of-house operations that are crucial to your business profitability. This involves HR and recruitment, training and development, social media, accounts and finances, emails and procedures, suppliers and costings.

Operational balance – You can break an operation or operator into three parts.

1. The doing part (making coffee).
2. The entrepreneurial part (the dreamer).
3. The practical part (the BOH operations).

It is important to have an equal balance of all these three; the failure of one will cause another to fail. Each part will try to win over the other at various stages, but with planning and discipline you can maintain the balance.

Making your business into a product – One day, hopefully, someone will want to buy your business, or perhaps one day you will wish to sell it, just like you want to sell a cup of coffee. So you make that coffee as delicious and as attractive as possible in order to attract buyers, as you should with your business. The problem is, you may only ever get one chance to do so, and so you need to make it as valuable as possible for when that time arrives. This means working on every single part of the business, so that the value of it keeps rising and rising. Put yourself in the buyer's shoes: What would you want the business to be if you were going to pay for it? What would you pay for your business/product?

JOHNNY – SIDE STORY

I could teeter on the edge of sycophancy with Peter. I'd always been a huge admirer of his business and decided to ask him for an interview to share with some of our coaching clients. Peter has always been generous in his praise for our first book, but this wasn't what drove me to undertake the interview.

The London coffee scene was just starting to explode at the time Peter started Kaffeine and I could see that he was not just jumping on the bandwagon. I knew he was not only winning awards but also making money. That may sound glib and obvious, but for many of the very cool cafés that opened around that time it simply wasn't the case.

As Peter says here, you must realise that this is a business, and a very serious business at that. We've been preaching this since day one in our books, seminars, consulting and coaching but it is still something that is so often not faced up to when people venture into the industry.

Peter's café in Great Titchfield Street is consistently the one café I send potential new entrants to visit. Often they will explain to me that they love various other coffee shops in London and how they'd like to model them. Quite often I know that these, sometimes über cool, coffee shops aren't making any money or are barely surviving. I send them to Kaffeine so they can grasp how busy a tiny little shop can be and observe just how wonderful a mix of food and astonishing coffee Peter produces.

If you haven't visited Kaffeine then I heartily recommend you do so. Nearly always you'll see Peter there and it's worth observing the astonishing level of detail he puts in. A visit to Kaffeine requires you to be observant and notice how all these details work together. Watch how the food is presented, the coffee and items such as mint tea are served; observe the efficient use of space behind the counter.

Finally, make sure you check out Peter's blog at www.kaffeinelondon.blogspot.co.uk. It's a wonderful insight, right back to the opening, of how the business has grown as well as the growing pains of the new store.

I'm not alone in my respect for Peter – he is incredibly generous with his time and has worked with numerous employees to help them set up on their own, as well as younger operators from other parts of the country.

You'll not be surprised to know that Peter sent me his answers on an immaculately branded email attachment, using his correct font and with the precise number of words written as the email title. There's a lesson there, too . . .

HUGO – SIDE STORY

I love models and this is in my view simply the best execution I have ever seen of a coffee shop business. Complete awareness and understanding of every detail means Peter is the supreme coffee entrepreneur. I always wished that Kaffeine would serve filter coffee because I knew it would be as close to perfect as you could get and one day Peter explained precisely, as ever, that he didn't serve it because of space, speed and consistency issues. The right decision for his customers, staff and the business. Knowing when not to do something takes courage, vision and a deep understanding of the why.

However, he serves fabulous batch-brewed filter coffee at Middlesex County Cricket Club, brewed perfectly to Gold Cup standards.

Peter Dore-Smith's one-sentence takeaway
Make your business into a product.

PHILIP ASH

Coffee Cure

Philip is the owner of four coffee shops in Bangor, County Down. Coffee Cure is an eclectic mix of a superb suburban coffee shop, a large, traditional and strongly food-based café, an incredibly busy coffee stall within beautiful gardens, and a drive-through. His business has grown rapidly as a result of some exceptional insight and negotiating skills for sites that might not normally be seen as workable.

www.coffeecureni.com

What is the one thing you wish you'd known before you started?

I wish I'd known how to manage staff better. In the early days the business totally dominated my life. I'd gone from complete freedom at the weekends with my property business to a situation where I knew I was highly likely to get a call at some stage on a Sunday that would necessitate me having to stop whatever I was doing and go in and work. There was always somebody sick, hungover or who simply didn't turn up.

It was my own fault, obviously – in my previous businesses we'd always had managers who had taken up this slack, but with Coffee Cure I didn't have the budget for this and wanted to learn the business from the ground up. The staff were badly organised and I had very little flexibility with those I did employ. They were nearly all full time, so there was no slack in the system to help in times of need – I was the slack . . . and in the beginning, that had a very large and negative impact on me and my family.

Nowadays, I've built a staff structure with much more support and flexibility. I still work hands-on in our various outlets, nearly every day of the week, but there is control and a structure, which means I can have a life outside the business.

What, in your opinion, is the secret to success of your business and great coffee shops and cafés in general?

For me the biggest secret is customer relations. That sounds simple, but really what I mean is knowing the names and as many facts as possible about the customer. I'm dreadful at remembering names but knew that it was a critical part of the business and so made a big effort, especially in the early days, to not let this hold me back. I bought a simple black notebook from the local convenience store and kept it under the till.

For every new customer I would, in as hopefully a seamless way as possible, try and find out critical facts about them and their lives. Did they like football, and if so what team did they support? If not football, what other sports did they follow? Did they travel and if so where had they been recently or would they like to visit? Did they have kids or grand kids? What were their names and what did they do or enjoy?

I'd then scribble these notes in my little book with a page for each customer. Even if I hadn't managed to get their name, I'd scribble enough to give me a point of reference when they came back in. It might initially read something like: *Grey hair, glasses, walks with a limp. Supports Liverpool.*

And then I'd build on that over time. What this allowed me to do was greet them as an old friend the next time they came in. I rarely remembered the specifics, but once I'd made their coffee I'd duck under the till, find their entry in the book and then be able to address the details, perhaps only very briefly, when I took their coffee or food over to them.

These days I rarely have to consult the book, but it was absolutely pivotal to the success of the business in the early days – I collected at least 200 names and details in that book and have sought to transfer these principles through to all my staff in all the businesses we now have. It works particularly well in a suburban store, but the core principle applies to all our sites and all hospitality in general.

Secondly, and I know this is an obvious one, but quality and, perhaps more importantly, consistency of coffee is vital. We relentlessly train our staff and keep tasting to ensure that we're hitting those targets. Before I started in the industry, I had no idea how many variables there were in the production of a great cup of coffee. Thankfully, I love and am obsessive about that side of the business, but it's something you can never take for granted. One of my biggest challenges is to ensure that all staff know that 'if it's not right throw it out'. Employees so often feel they're doing you a favour and saving money by handing out coffee that is 'almost right', but nothing could be further from the truth.

My business is built almost entirely on ensuring we have repeat customers, and just one poor coffee can severely dent that objective. Two or three in a row and you're leaving yourself wide open to losing that customer for good.

We have multiple 'seven days a week' customers and this forms the rock-solid foundations of what we do. Some of the older generation even visit twice a day. The staff know the value of these people and treat them accordingly. In many cases when these staff leave for new jobs or to travel or go to university, the regulars will give them gifts. We want to become part of the lives of our customers – to be genuine friends.

At Christmas I'll treat some of my best customers in our neighbourhood store to a Christmas dinner, with wine, at our more food-based outlet in the centre of the town. I know exactly what these customers mean to my livelihood, so I work very hard to make sure they understand how much I appreciate them.

I think it's vital to remember that we're in the hospitality business as much as the business of mechanically making a great product. I work very hard at this but I think it has to be instinctive, something you'd do anyway. You can't always be expecting something back from what you might do to improve a customer's day.

Recently we had a bin lorry pull up outside the store and three bin men came in and ordered their coffees to take away. I noticed they took them outside and sat in their lorry drinking them. Obviously they were worried that they might be too dirty to sit inside.

We operate a top-up policy for our coffees. There are always pros and cons to this system but for me it works well, allowing me to build up the relationships that I know are so important to the success of the business. Obviously some people do take advantage of it, but if you can pleasantly and assertively lay out the ground rules then it usually works well.

On the day the bin men were sitting in their lorry, I was doing my round with the coffee pot and decided to go outside and see if they wanted a top-up, too. When I opened the door they looked shocked. They thought I wanted some help removing some extra rubbish or even to ask them to move on and not create an eyesore outside my shop. I laughed and simply told them that I was topping up the coffees inside and they were just as entitled to it as anyone else.

These guys now come back on a very regular basis and we have a second bin lorry that visits us now, too. The advantage here is more than a few extra coffee sales – they eat a lot more than my average customer, so I get to increase my average spend – the holy grail for any of us in this business. But the key point here is that I didn't offer those top-ups to them with the expectation that they'd come back more often or tell their friends. I simply did it because I want happy customers and felt they shouldn't be at a disadvantage.

JOHNNY – SIDE STORY

Philip is a good friend of mine and I helped him with his business in the initial stages. But he's one of those guys who takes the baton and runs with it. You give him an idea or a concept and he'll make sure it happens. He'll find solutions. That's refreshing and very rare in the people I help and consult with.

So when he told me about his solution for remembering names in his black book, I loved it. At that stage (maybe six months after he'd opened his first site) we roughly counted that he had about one hundred names in the book. I was due to produce a marketing seminar at Caffè Culture that year and we produced a list of fifty-five specific ways to better market coffee shops and cafés. I instinctively knew that Philip's 'a hundred names in a black book' strategy would make the final cut.

On the day, we had approximately a hundred people in the room and Hugh and I delivered our fifty-five strategies to a generally very appreciative crowd. Afterwards we did a survey with Caffè Culture to see whether people felt they got value. The answer was a resounding, but not emphatic, yes. We had two complainants. Both felt that we covered too many issues we'd dealt with before. Neither wanted their money back or were properly unhappy, but both wanted to make sure that we were aware of this.

Initially, I bristled at this – I went through the slides and worked out that out of the fifty-five methods we discussed there were only twenty that we'd mentioned in previous books. I was genuinely concerned that we maybe hadn't provided the value we'd hoped and intended to give, but the facts seemed to back up that we really had provided a lot of new content, almost all of which was proven in our own businesses or with those of clients.

So I decided to ask one of the unhappy attendees directly for some more feedback. Since I'd literally just put in Philip's 'Create a black book with a hundred names and interests' strategy in at the last minute I knew that was completely fresh content – so I asked the attendee whether he'd heard about that before. He admitted that, no, he hadn't. But then listed reasons why it wouldn't work for his business and how he could never get his staff to do that.

I then listed a list of other tactics that we'd shown, and in almost every case he came up with reasons as to why he couldn't put that in the business or why it wouldn't work for him.

In our consulting work we find two very distinct categories of people. On the one side you have people, like Philip, who take everything you tell them and find a way to make it work. But they also take a broader and more strategic view – they take a wider look at the information you provide and find their own solutions and tactics to create a solution.

On the other side you find people who find all sorts of reasons to stay in the status quo – to blame the economy, their staff, location, their memory for names, suppliers, equipment – the list is endless. And sadly, these are the people that almost always fail.

Philip Ash's one-sentence takeaway

Never forget this is about hospitality; it's about serving people in an environment that makes them want to return – it's never just about a great cup of coffee or sandwich.

REBECCA STONE

The Bottle Kiln

The Bottle Kiln at West Hallam is a family business, started thirty years ago and run by Becky and her brother Nic. Nic looks after the retail side and Becky runs the café. It is based on the site of a unique renovated old pottery with a landmark bottle-neck kiln at its centre. It is a beautiful place, lovingly restored and incorporating a Japanese garden as well as the retail areas (home furnishings, cards, jewellery, toiletries, accessories and so on) and the café, both of which have won national awards. It is a place where people meet up, shop, eat and drink and, most importantly, relax and get away from the stressful world outside.

http://bottlekiln.co.uk

What is the one thing you wish you'd known before you started?

Before you open, fully understand the massive commitment you are taking on. You need to have an incredibly busy business to actually make any money – and that takes a lot of physical work.

And having a fool's guide to the inevitable banana skins that you will slip up on in the first year, as these are quite often the defining things that make or break you. Like making sure you know the exact point you need to be paying VAT, employing your first members of staff, interviewing through to sorting out wages etc.

What do you believe is the secret to success of your business and great coffee shops and cafés in general?

Location

We are situated in a large village roughly halfway between Nottingham and Derby, and about twenty minutes' drive from each. Though not an especially prosperous area as such, we are within easy drive of many villages and city suburbs that contain very well-to-do people. The site itself is attractive, well maintained and on a main A-road. And, of course, the bottle kiln itself is well known as a landmark and helps guide new people in.

Products

Baking all of our own products straight away makes us unique; if a customer likes our food they cannot find it anywhere else. We are in control of the freshness, deliciousness and most importantly margins on price. In catering you have to sell a lot of food to make a good living, so if it's not great you won't sell it through. If a customer loves your location, ambience and freshly baked product, price will not be an issue.

I make sure that I know every recipe and have them typed out and in folders for staff. I keep expanding, refining and most importantly training, which means the options for customers are always improving and moving forward. I spend time pricing all items carefully and know my margins. Look for great products that customers love and keep them FRESH! If it's a scone, I make sure they are sold on that day – do not compromise!

I spend time visiting other businesses for inspiration and to get a feeling for what's on-trend or interesting to adapt to my own customer base.

Creating a full and exciting counter with WOW displays, good signage and plenty of colour is important. Cooking your own food also means the place smells good, immediately giving customers the right signals. Being aware of the changing needs of customers, especially things like gluten-free products, means you can quickly build up a whole new customer base just by providing delicious products for people with dietary requirements, which leads to lots of good will for the business.

Adding value to a product, such as a delicious biscuit to accompany your interestingly sourced loose-leaf tea in a branded tea pot, gives you a very high margin as well as a unique product that customers will love. Just bake some delicious shortbread biscuits fresh each morning, place them on your tea cup and saucer and watch the customers come flooding back for more.

Branding

We have spent a lot of time focusing on branding the business, starting with choosing great colour combinations that speak to the right customer base for us in a very positive way.

I feel that you can tell so much from a simple sign – what a business is going to give just from the colour and font used.

We have a very creative lady on board that works on our branding, whether that's signage around the building, websites, handouts, menus, Facebook, Twitter or photography. She's constantly readdressing the branding and keeping a great energy and flow throughout the business. I feel that the customers can totally buy into the brand and love taking a little or a lot of it away with them.

Senses

Keeping the business looking great is so important and that starts in the car park with good landscaping, plus signage and the exterior of buildings. Internally refreshing the colours, wallpaper and lighting, and using craftsmen to create interesting furnishings that are unique, I constantly reinvest to keep the appearance of the building fresh and exciting.

I think about the smells of the business; if you bake your own products, even from the car park customers will pick up a delicious smell. Coffee, bread, cakes and savoury lunch items all create great smells. Avoiding those that have a negative smell, such as pancakes!

The acoustics of a building are so important too: make sure the furnishings are soft enough to make the inside space comfortable on the ears. Play relaxing background music and be careful not to have a lot of negative industrial noises – a coffee machine can be good; a dishwasher not so good.

Make sure all of the flavours are good, whether it's a well-extracted coffee or a delicious salad, never letting the standards drop.

Cleanliness is also very important, especially areas like the toilets. Invest in great soaps (something as simple as that gives a huge message to a customer) and bring in a good cleaner, giving them enough time to thoroughly clean the whole business.

Loyalty

If customers love your business they can't wait to tell everyone; if they are indifferent they will ignore you; if they hate you they also can't wait to tell everyone, so you need to be in the love area.

I definitely invest in goodwill, which can be loyalty cards, vouchers for local charities, fetes etc. We have a 'no questions asked money back' or exchange for any unsatisfactory item policy, offer free coffees to ease difficult situations, look after customers that might struggle, e.g. with prams, or elderly people, and respond positively to criticism. You can completely turn a negative situation around just by listening to a customer and letting them know you CARE.

A simple thing like a free coffee can cost you pence but gain you thousands of pounds in return visits, not only from the customer who receives it but through all of the positive stories they will tell to other potential customers. Likewise, a branded voucher donated to a well-attended event can reach so many potential customers and be more productive than an expensive advert placed in a magazine.

Encourage your staff to always welcome back the regular customers and embrace the new ones. And move the business slowly forward to constantly engage the regular customers.

People

Running a café long-term successfully is all about the people. You have to enjoy, respect and treat people fairly. Your staff need to be as loyal as your customers! They have to buy 100 per cent into the bones of the business and be proud of what they help to create. This way you can retain them and keep them positive. I feel that it takes at least a year for staff to properly understand the job, so constant changes of staff can be one of the biggest stresses in a business.

Taking time to find and employ great staff might be painful, but it's so important. Liking the people that you work with and knowing that they will fit into your existing team is crucial.

I find students are a great source of staffing; by interviewing at sixteen, you can check whether they are going to go to university locally and then potentially retain them for up to six years or more. Mums ready for a part-time work can also become a brilliant, strong part of your team. Fill your business with bright, interesting people that totally want to push the business forward.

Having good relationships with suppliers is so important: being loyal and fair with them ensures that they will take time to look after your business.

Money

It's too easy to let the detail of the money become secondary to all the immediate issues, but try not to let it, otherwise you're not running a business – it's running you!

My overheads are reviewed at least once a year to ensure the best rates we can get on electricity etc. We own the property, so don't have huge rents to find.

Wages are the biggest expenditure, mainly because we cook all of our own food, which I believe gives us the great margins that balance out the extra wage expense.

I know exactly what my wages are per day with an uplift of holiday and sickness pay, and know exactly where I want them to be as a percentage of net takings. I take the time to make these percentages work well for the business

Working out expenditure of products used in a week, and working on keeping the percentages as tight as possible, along with understanding that keeping these two figures tight and under control, is where the profit is.

Keeping control of tight ordering and wastage is a great focus. I get staff to work from written recipes and price those recipes with good margins, addressing this yearly to take into consideration price increases. I change the prices on my menu every year without fail and at the same time increase wages.

It's important to constantly re-invest in the business to keep everything flowing forward. This can be equipment, training, branding, maintenance, re-designing etc.

Passion

I feel that I am on a journey and nowhere near reaching the end – there are so many more things to learn and achieve. Running a successful business needs huge determination and energy; if you lose that it's a backwards journey.

Changing the business in small ways needs to happen on a regular basis; big changes should happen a couple of times a year; and fundamentally huge changes perhaps every five years or else, I think, you're slipping backwards!

You need to be passionate about success, whether it's winning a competition or gaining your environmental health 5-standard rating, being a great accountant, public relations person, main-tenance man, interior decorator, first-aider or cook . . . the hats you wear are endless.

Let all of the people around you know what your standards are and pull them all along with your enthusiasm.

This could all equal SUCCESS!

JOHNNY – SIDE STORY

I had the great pleasure of working with Becky over the course of a year and her business is a wonderful example of success through meticulous hard graft. You'll notice that she has an incredible eye for the detail of the customer journey – this is a constant process within the business – including learning the lesson about pancake smells. Far too often owners don't fully consider the wider ramifications of certain changes or new items on the menu.

The creation of high-value product combinations, which are also high margin, is something that is often overlooked, but it lies at the core of any menu development strategy that we work with. Becky is a master of this. She creates incredibly delicious food but has a very focused hand on the margin calculator at the same time.

She also makes great use of sampling, one of the cheapest and most effective marketing tools out there.

Rebecca Stone's one-sentence takeaway

Do not compromise – and make sure your staff buy 100 per cent into your vision.

SÉ GORMAN

Café Krem

From a restaurant and pub background Sé Gorman started a coffee business in Newry, Northern Ireland, expanding to seven sites and juggling the good, the bad and the ugly. He and his employees have been multiple national barista champions, judges and specialist coffee experts for twenty years. He still operates the original site along with four kiosks and cart sites in Belfast.

www.cafekrem.com

What is the one thing you wish you'd known before you started?

If I were to pick one general area of concern I think I would go for attention to detail in each area. To go into specific detail about something almost always holds somebody (and yourself) accountable and provides the measurement that is required to make good decisions. This might sound obvious but it means measuring the gram drop from your grinder, every time, tasting the twentieth flapjack out of the oven to make sure it is right, checking there are no crumbs under tables that have just been vacated, turning up and being open on time every time, and such like.

Luckily, the one thing I decided to focus on from the start was making my core product coffee. It's the one that will make you the most money. In my case I never lost sight of that, and everything else was an ancillary.

What do you believe is the secret to success of your business and great coffee shops and cafés in general?

This business is primarily about execution. So much time is taken up with doing 'the right thing' and by that I mean quality coffee, great taste, wonderful service, customer engagement, added value and many, many more details, as I said above. However, a real awareness of 'the commercial thing' is what I believe to be equally important. One drives your business while the other makes money that allows you to advance.

Keep trying new ways to sell the profitable lines but manage the cost of failure; fail fast, fail cheap, move on to the next idea. Don't use ideas from your competitors; adapt ideas from outside your industry. Look at the quirky opportunities that won't suit the big boys, identify the local need and see how you can fulfil it at a profit.

Listen to everyone but be selective in what you actually hear. Constructive criticism is a million times more valuable than praise.

Make sure the people you employ understand and share your vision; it's a bonus if they have the same passion. Employ people for their competencies not just because you like them, and be aware their differences can add value to the company. Humility and generosity are good things.

Everything you do is communicating your brand, so don't do anything wrong. Always view your business as a customer sees it. This allows you to concentrate on the details. Don't make it difficult in any way for customers to spend their hard-earned cash with you. Get out and interact with people who are not your customers and understand why this is.

Remember, an exit strategy is not necessary, but a profitable strategy is.

An effective leader is much more valuable than a charismatic one, and it may not always be you.

Take care of yourself and don't get locked into patterns. I try to be emotionally self-aware, to take care of myself physically – good nutrition, enough sleep, regular exercise. It's also important to maintain my social connections, friends and relationships. Intellectually and spiritually I try to maintain my learning capacity and mental agility and to hold on to a purpose in life.

And above all, have fun – otherwise it'll all go Pete Tong.

JOHNNY – SIDE STORY

I've never had a conversation with Sé that I didn't enjoy. His knowledge of coffee surpasses mine by a mile, but he's also a hardcore 'let's give this a try' entrepreneur. Like most of us, he has learned the hard way that the streets of specialty coffee aren't guaranteed to be paved with gold, but his passionate desire to keep producing great coffee and food is what the business is built on. There's some great wisdom in his contribution.

HUGO – SIDE STORY

I remember Sé walking into my training rooms many, many years ago and saying that he was opening a coffee bar and had been told to talk to me by Mark McMurray. This is always a way to get somebody's attention since Mark is a fantastic character and in my opinion a referral like this is the holy grail of marketing.

We immediately got on well and while I helped Sé in the early days, his interest and passion for coffee brought him and his fantastic team the Northern Ireland Barista Championship title in the form of a Krem barista for the best part of a decade. He went on to judge national competitions and is highly respected by many, opening a magnificently innovative Brew Bar two years ahead of its time in Belfast and closing because the market just wasn't ready. He has many fans and followers – just not enough to sustain required revenues.

I would have to say that he now helps me significantly more than I help him. A constant quality controller as a customer and a candid contributor to our roast-to-order and origin stock holding, as well as a steady, trustworthy and loyal friend, makes this coffee relationship probably the most significant of any.

People like Sé are gold dust because they keep you right, build you up and knock some humility into you when it's required – interestingly, usually always at the precise required moment, rarely before and never after. Both Sé and Krem are special finds, ones that should always be sought after.

Sé Gorman's one-sentence takeaway

Candor requires the ability to advise without ranting or preaching. Sé would always end a good piece of advice with the phrase 'Just Sayin'" – plus that smile.

SONJA BJÖRK GRANT

Kaffibrugghúsið (Coffee Brewery)

Sonja is an entrepreneur, barista and roaster. She is one of the pioneers of World Barista Championship and a past chairwoman of World Coffee Events (WCE) Advisory board. Sonja travels around the world, giving talks, seminars and creating workshops related to training and judging. She has also owned and operated coffee-bar businesses in Iceland.

What is the one thing you wish you'd known before you started?

There were not many things that surprised me in a negative way when I started my simple business, apart from how heavy the system was around licensing. After four months of fighting the system and paperwork, the licence was on the wall in a frame.

Maybe it would have been good to know about the bank crisis . . . but someone was already using the crystal ball when I got the idea of starting my own business. It was very exciting to start a business just after the crisis. Coffee is the cheapest luxury money can buy and creates a fun atmosphere, bringing people together to talk or just enjoy cups of all kinds of flavours. Endless possibilities.

What do you believe is the secret to success of your business and great coffee shops and cafés in general?

The secret

The secret behind my business is not really a secret – it was very simple. I wanted to continue to train myself as a coffee professional, and to add to my knowledge. One way to do that was to form a coffee company. To have fun in learning and brewing coffee was the one of the most important items; the other was passion. It's impossible to run a fun and inspiring coffee company without huge dose of passion.

I was ready to jump into the hard work of being my own boss and open the first third-wave coffee shop in Iceland: a 6kg pink shop roaster in the middle of the coffee shop, a few tables for guests, and I held seminars in the evening after closing time. A simple idea.

My background of running coffee shops, training baristas, quality control and giving lectures made the startup easier.

And the fact that Iceland was bank robbed three months before I opened, helped in many ways. I'm not saying it was easy – it was hell, but in a creative way, and many good things and ideas came out of the bank crisis. We were a community in that small third-wave coffee company.

The staff

One of the successes, I think, is that most of my staff were working with me because they wanted to learn more about coffee. So every day we experimented with brewing, grinding and roasting. Training ourselves into becoming better professionals. I know they liked the freedom, and because this was a small workplace, all of them were drivers; there were no spare passengers.

The coffee guests

I was lucky that because of the location of the company it was easy to attract a huge group of regular customers, around 75–80 per cent. For my business, retailing was a good part of the daily income, and my customers started to become aware of the freshness of the coffee each time. I had a simple recycling system where the customers brought their own coffee cups or vessels for a refill of coffee beans. We didn't have discount cards, but bringing your own coffee cup and coffee bean vessel meant they paid around 30p less for each drink or bag of beans. My customers really liked this system of bringing back the coffee bags for a refill. They had an environmentally friendly awareness, plus my business saved some hundreds of unused coffee bags.

The business is not a pop-up growth; it is long-term journey with great relationships, from the farmer to the cup in front of the coffee customer.

To have a character

The focus of my company was to make it simple and transparent. But also to think outside the box – to look at what kind of coffee shops there were already in Iceland, and do the opposite.

We used what we owned – for example, all the furniture came from friends and family and the accessories were collected from all around the coffee world. The vinyl record player was popular, with the table next to it controlling the music and able to play whatever they wanted. The tables were only five or so, forcing people to sit together, and some great new relationships came out of the trip to the coffee shop.

The coffee relationship

In small communities it is sometimes difficult to change old habits and my idea was to shake things up. So the new thing in Iceland in 2008 was to offer a single-origin light roast for espresso. And having only coffee from two farmers at the time meant that guests were aware of where the coffee was coming from and interested in knowing more about the farmers and their processing.

For me, being a part of the coffee industry is life itself. Coffee gives me energy, not only as drink but also from the culture that surrounds it, which is full of colour and flavour. The relationship and journey from the farmer to the coffee customer is amazing and full of exciting possibilities.

HUGO – SIDE STORY

Everybody in the coffee world knows and loves Sonja. She is one of life's seriously good people, tirelessly devoting her time to the cause and the benefit of other people. Her answers to our questions are so typical and honest of her, and as a result so insightful. About character, colour, relationships and, of course, other people – her staff and the customer. She has led judging panels, advised and coached baristas from around the world as well as led her beloved Icelandic teams in every competition ever established. An undoubted champion of the coffee world with immense knowledge, Sonja is the real deal.

Sonja Björk Grant's one-sentence takeaway

Community – if you ensure you create a great guest culture and become a valued member of the community (on all levels), your chances of success are improved enormously.

STEPHEN HURST

Mercanta

Stephen Hurst is a very special Coffee Hunter. He is founder of Mercanta: The Coffee Hunters, one of the world's leading specialty green coffee brokers. He began life in the coffee trading division of Goldman Sachs and has served on the board of directors of the Alliance for Coffee Excellence (non-profit owners of the Cup of Excellence programme) and the Specialty Coffee Association of Europe's board. He later founded London School of Coffee, which became a sister company involved in the training, consultancy and education sector of the specialty coffee business. He owns a coffee farm in Brazil, and operates several offices around the world in London, Seattle and Singapore.

www.coffeehunter.com

What is the one thing you wish you'd known before you started?

There are three things I remember from the early days of Mercanta's business. Things I would put in the category of I **Wish I Had Known**:

1. Partner
2. Personnel
3. Paymaster C

Let's call this the three **P**s:

My original business **partner** was a guy I'd known in a supplier/buyer relationship and also as a friend. But this did not make for a good business partnership. I bought him out (paid him back) within less than two years of establishing Mercanta. When he received his part of the original investment (a not inconsiderable sum), he phoned me and said, 'My God, I don't believe you paid me back the investment. I would have never have paid you.' I said, that's why we are not partners. Mercanta could have been folded up and simply re-started in a new guise, but that wasn't the correct way to go. It cost me a lot to make that point but the simple ethics of that laid the foundation of the good business that Mercanta has become. There is simply a right way to do things, but it is not necessarily the easiest way.

I hired an expensive **personnel** agency to find an employee in the early days, a sales person. I paid the employment agency a handsome sum, money we could not afford at that early stage. The guy left after a year. Bad call. Find your own staff if you can, or at least wait until you can afford to call in the agencies

Paymaster would be called Finance except that does not start with P. We had a bank loan facility that was ill suited to our business, a use it or pay anyway feature. The bank needed to set aside this considerable line for our funding, so if we did not use the facility we paid anyway. This led to us getting involved in dubious or marginal business just to create the churn or usage of the available credit line. We paid another fine sum to get OUT OF that deal. All lending comes with strings attached whether from the bank, family, friends, or PayDayLender.com.

Understand very clearly and thoroughly the expectations (financial and operational) of anyone who is lending your business money. Get this straight.

Those three things I would do differently. However, the bad business partner did send an assistant to work with me in the early days. This 'assistant' later became my business partner, and absolutely essential in the formative years of Mercanta. Flori was instrumental in the development of our business. My point here being the Silver Lining theory – something initially very negative actually had a very positive outcome.

As our business grew we still had the two steps forward, two steps back feeling – Flori and I knew coffee, we were making some headway in a market that really did not exist when we set up.

In the first Cup of Excellence Auction, I thought, selling premium-priced raw materials sounded like an interesting idea as nobody was doing it. The auction is public domain internet based. We paid, I recall, say $1.50/lb for one of the lots in the first Cup of Excellence auction. That is about the cost of today's commodity price, perhaps twice the price of the commodity price at the time. People took time out to phone and mock us the next day.

'What clowns would pay $1.50/lb for Brazil when the market price was half that?' they said. Idiots!

We lost money on that business but discovered a programme that transformed the landscape of specialty coffee. I served on the Alliance for Coffee Excellence Board voluntarily for eight years. An ironic aside to this story is the fool who phoned me to mock us later asked for a job at Mercanta. I guess you know what happened to that enquiry.

So many people find it much easier to follow than lead; I have tremendous respect for those genuine pioneers who did something against the grain, something genuinely innovative in whatever field. Hundreds of companies have copied our model now. At least one of them had the (discrete) integrity and honesty to tell me shamelessly that they copied our business model in setting up a competitor.

One other salient lesson came from the early days. One day a letter came in, offering a free trial consultation with a management consultant. I am the last man to want to waste my money on some psychobabble nonsense from a person who is clueless about our business. But what the hell, we thought. The first consultation was free and, well, we were getting desperate.

This cracker came in to see us, without the least idea about specialty coffee, telling us things about the business we did not want to hear. I wanted to throw him out.

But this man became an investor, a good friend, and he set us straight. His wife also came to work for us. We knew coffee, we knew the market, we knew too much. Our consultant told us some harsh home truths and he was right. He was a new set of eyes, not weighed down by any preconceived ideas. A man with vast business experience internationally who knew business, and some business truths. The fact he did not initially know coffee was a blessing. This is the (We Can't See the) Woods Through the Trees theory.

Lately, some of the most successful businesses we have seen are NOT run by coffee people. This coffee expertise they 'buy in' – sourcing, roasting, blending, logistics, risk management. These 'non-coffee' coffee businesses concentrate on the facts, sales, their clients, marketing, brand building.

At least 20–30 per cent of the start-up roasters (and now also some importers) we see today are lifestyle 'enterprises'. They are not businesses, but rather like breweries; owning a coffee roastery is the latest accessory. Owners want to travel all over the world, put together small inefficient purchases, so they claim to buy direct (even though frequently this direct purchase is actually imported and financed by a third party), spending valuable time and resources on everything but actually selling and building the business with THEIR customers. Obsessed or fanatic about coffee, some of these new startups are genuine people, dedicated, and enthusiastic, but their efforts are ill placed. Independently funded by inheritances, trust funds, rich relatives or another previous successful business, these lifestyle players are now quite prevalent in the specialty coffee landscape.

What do you believe is the secret to success of your business and great coffee shops and cafés in general?

The Secret: I am tempted to think up something astounding and remarkable, but some or a lot of the secret is simply hard work. I know a lot of people work hard and get nowhere, so let me try to examine some of the facts which led to our success.

Focus. We did not bend in the wind of trends (Fairtrade, Rainforest, capsules, Nespresso, etc). These are all important sectors but nothing has been a category killer in coffee; if anything it is ever more fragmented. Focus, stay on the path. Our message has been all about quality from day one and we don't have little asterisks and footnotes to say 'except when'.

Good Business is good business. Deal fairly and honestly with people. My original business partner was just not on the same lines. I could have thrown him under a bus, disappeared, or just re-started the business in a new name. No. Do it properly. Deal with people properly, with integrity and fairness. We pay high prices for fine coffee, not for charity but because if the quality producer survives and thrives we may well do, too. Our success is the success of the producer and roaster allied to us; it is mutually beneficial, not 'we make money at your expense' – quite the opposite, in fact.

Brutal hard work. I know a lot of people put in the hours and end up nowhere, but really this is PART of the whole picture. Working harder, working longer, working better.

It's still all about the people. Technology, social networks, communications' revolution – it's still all about The People. It's personal. I used to know all the producers we bought from and roasters we sold to: Are you really going to rip the guy off whose house you just stayed in? Are you really at that barbeque drinking and laughing to turn the people over a week later?

It's still about the people (part 2). Staff, partners, employees, rise and fall within this group. Get your hiring right at least 80 per cent of the time; you will never or rarely get 100 per cent. A bad employee, business partner or associate will kill you – waste your time, money, energy and resources. It's the oldest one in the book: hire good people. We did, and now having trained them up to our in-house standards, real estate agents, pharma salesmen, charity workers, coffee geeks, chemistry graduates, engineers, wine merchants and baristas can all get jobs when and where they want because the Mercanta name is on their CV.

HUGO – SIDE STORY

'Hurstyboy', as the Brazilians I stayed with call Stephen, is a one-off. He taught me the value of relationships, real relationships as opposed to those that we all need in business. Stephen buys from people who love him and without a doubt he has made the coffee world a better place. Enough said. His ability to stand up and be counted is what made the difference and I for one, and anybody else selling speciality agricultural beverages, should want to hear what he has to say – always. Well, almost!

Stephen Hurst's one-sentence takeaway

People: understand that you can never survive without understanding what makes people tick and surround yourself with the best – at every level of your business.

STEPHEN LEIGHTON

Has Bean

Stephen Leighton has transformed the UK coffee scene and has grown his Has Bean coffee-roasting business in the last ten years to enviable proportions. His passion and drive is there for all to see. As an early adopter, he has maximised the use of technology to connect with so many people globally, and with more than 300 episodes of *In My Mug* and dozens of blogs, audiobooks, *Tamper Tantrums* events and videos, he is unsurpassed in the information that he provides. The Michael Buffer of coffee, he is the go-to WBC and event host.

www.hasbean.co.uk

What is the one thing you wish you'd known before you started?

How do you answer a question like this? I wish I knew everything that has got me to the point I'm at now, but if I had known them would I be in the position? I believe we learn lots from our lack of knowledge and mistakes.

It's a little-known fact that I began my first three years in coffee with a coffee shop. The first coffee shop in Stafford (my home town). Not just the first independent, but before Starbucks and Costa had even put a pin in their map of the county town of 70,000 people. I opened my door and spent the first two weeks explaining what an espresso was, and how cappuccino was just milky coffee with a bit of froth.

By the third week I was in a panic; I had no money to 'burn' in this shop. I'd used every penny I had to get it open and the till wasn't ringing. I tried to teach a whole town single handily what coffee was. The small coffee roaster in the corner just blew their mind, and talk of seeds not beans; the fact that coffee arrives in green bean form grown by real people the other side of the world, made them look at me like an alien that had just landed from Mars.

So I changed, I dumbed down, I sold just coffee, mugs of tea, sandwiches, soup, jacket potatoes and became like every other café in town. I took every single customer's piece of advice: we sold Red Bull, Mars bars, jacket potatoes, salad and anything else they suggested. And with every item added to the menu, I felt a little sadder. A little more resentful of the shop and towards my customers. It wasn't their fault; it was all mine.

The one thing I learned that I brought into the roasting business, and I do until this very day, is to only sell things that make me happy. And if at any point it begins to make me unhappy, it gets dropped. A clear vision of where you want to be is imperative, and deviation from that plan has to be scrutinised and scrutinised again, and then reviewed and reviewed for happiness level. If it makes me happier then it's probably a good thing; if it doesn't then it's most likely not.

Now does that make you wealthy? No, but a happy business I tend to find does make you wealthy. So the one thing I wish I'd known (a long way around the houses) is that vision is everything, and changes should be evolutions not revolutions to the original plan.

What do you believe is the secret to success of your business and great coffee shops and cafés in general?

Am I successful and do I run a great coffee operation? I can point at many roasters who roast many times more tonnes than me. I can also point at many more roasters who make more money than me and are stronger financial operations. But neither of these were my original goal, my original vision. This is where you think I am being coy or shy or pretending that I believe I am not successful, but trust me I think I'm the very best at what I do, because I use my own measurement tools.

If you had asked me back in 2003 when I began the roasting part of my coffee career, what my vision and goals were, it would have been simple – I wrote them down. So let's go over these now . . .

1. Have the best coffee in the world
Everyone thinks they have the best coffee in the world. No one says, 'Well this stuff is OK we will take it'. But I think we have found some fairly good producers out there – not rock star growers, but producers no one had heard of until we found them, and they have gone on to become rock star growers. Critically acclaimed from our peers, we are the only roaster from 2009–14 to have a coffee used by a barista champion of their country in every World Barista Championship final. So I'm happy that our coffee is up there.

2. Pay the best prices I can to the world best producers
Easy one to achieve you would think, but to remain competitive and to achieve my later goals it was important to balance this

with business sense. But our producers seem to like dealing with us and this is normally 49 per cent about personality and 51 per cent how much you pay.

3. Have fun, make friends

Every day I enjoy what I do, every day is not work, it is a giggle. I have friends all over the world, real friends who I could call up and ask if I could sleep on their sofa, and they would say yes in a heartbeat. I love my job and I love my life, so a big tick here.

4. Travel the world buying coffee

I am still the only buyer in the business and it will remain this way for as long as I'm able. I love visiting different lands, learning more about coffee. My passport is full of stamps, and last year I took off more than sixty times. I think that makes me fairly well travelled now – another tick!

5. Have beer and food in the cupboard and a roof over my and my family's head

Something that's quite often overlooked is that to be sustainable you have to survive. Paying the best prices could mean that I don't have any left for me, and man cannot feast on fun and air travel alone.

6. Never stop learning

Every day I learn something new about coffee. I came from such a low knowledge base that it was inevitable I achieved this one, but it's important to not know all the answers, and to continue to push boundaries and take on new ideas. So from my own measures I guess I am successful – from yours I may not be – but these principles are the foundations of what I wanted to do and why I am where I am today.

JOHNNY – SIDE STORY

There is a very fine line, which nearly all owners will agree with, between dumbing down to what the customer tells you they want and sticking to your vision. It's a tightrope that we've all walked and all wobbled on.

Sadly, there is no simple answer.

HUGO – SIDE STORY

When I first met Stephen he was still employed in his prison-officer day job, but it was obvious that this guy was going places. Determined, focused and in love with his product, Steve had charisma and attitude.

I was online one night at a Gary Vaynerchuk webinar when he offered a guest slot to book buyers and Steve immediately bought fifty books on the promise that Gary would do a *Wine Library TV* show with him in London. It was brilliant PR and the episode was legendary because they held the show backstage and tasted Carl Sara's Pinot from the bottle. Typically irreverent and entertaining: this is Steve.

Steven Leighton's one-sentence takeaway
Create a business that makes you happy and which works for your broader ideals and goals in life.

STEPHEN MORRISSEY

Intelligentsia

Stephen is the Training and Communications Director at Intelligentsia. He won the World Barista Championship in 2008. He has since carved out a special place in the US coffee world via his work at Intelligentsia, who operate a dozen bars in Chicago, New York and Los Angeles. Stephen has judged and been part of both WBC and WCE and was a founder of Coffee Common which, as a cool collaboration of coffee experts, made its debut at TED 2011.

www.intelligentsiacoffee.com

What is the one thing you wish you'd known before you started?

It's hard to answer this in a concise manner. A career in coffee can draw on so many different disciplines: hospitality, operations, agronomy, marketing, communications, finance, global economics, construction, science, design and taste. I've had to build competencies in each of these areas, and I don't expect I'm a unique case. One of the things we find so charming about coffee is that juxtaposition of simplicity and immense complexity. It's just a roasted seed, that's ground and mixed with hot water – but we know it's so much more. I identify more as a generalist than a specialist, and as the challenges around realising specialty coffee are so varied, I wish I'd invested more time in developing a broader skill set in my formative years. Which is not to say that the six years I spent studying music in college was a complete waste.

What do you believe is the secret to success of your business or great coffee shops and cafés in general?

I think it's a lot of things – so here's a list:

- Reject complacency – assume everything is broken and always look for ways to improve.
- Opening is easy – the hard part is maintaining that same hyper attention to detail three years in.
- Treat your staff well – empower them, let them know your expectations, and don't hire your friends.
- Good customer service is everything – it's often more important than your product.
- Always be cleaning.
- Pay attention to the little things – if people spot small failures, how can they trust you on everything else.
- Do everything well – don't sell anything that you don't fully endorse.
- Build your own brand – don't try to leverage others (this is true for your beer provider, coffee provider, soda provider etc).
- Know your cost of goods.
- Build something that's personal, that you care deeply about – don't just look to copy and paste other people's seemingly successful models.

HUGO – SIDE STORY

I first met Stephen on a project in 2004 when he was that music student, and I immediately knew he was a superstar. His skills were his exceptional rapport and interest in the detail of a good cup of coffee.

What was particularly interesting to observe was how he kept challenging norms and the answers he was getting from those who were happy to stay where they were and not challenge themselves, who unlike him accepted where they were. Once again, he highlights that coffee is both simple and endlessly complex. This is something none of us should take for granted. You might expect Stephen to be a preparation detail person, given his huge success as barista, but his list of 'secrets to success' extends way beyond coffee skills and it's no surprise that he is now working at a very high level in what is often regarded as one of the finest coffee shop chains in the world.

Stephen Morrissey's one-sentence takeaway

Opening is easy – the hard part is maintaining that same hyper attention to detail three years in.

WILLIAM FARMER

The Bay Tree

William is the owner of The Bay Tree in Holywood County Down. The Bay Tree is a coffee house/restaurant, which has become famous, on worldwide basis, for their cinnamon scones. William also operates an innovative project with farmer Joel Kerr called Farm and Food, where they hold special events in The Bay Tree highlighting and celebrating the process from farm to fork. The breeds they use for these evenings are allowed to grow at their own pace, stress free and without relying on grain feed.

www.baytreeholywood.co.uk

What is the one thing you wish you'd known before you started?

The ability to compose myself, take a step back and think a situation through. I used to react to a difficult situation immediately and rashly. Staff or supply issues will generally work out fine if you tackle them calmly and patiently. There's always a solution. Not that a good whinge doesn't feel good sometimes!

What do you believe is the secret to success of your business and great coffee shops and cafés in general?

We try not to be complacent. We've been around for more than twenty years and have established a strong reputation for consistently good food, but it's not something we would ever want to take for granted. We constantly research what's being cooked around the country (and beyond), we listen to what our customers are asking for and we try to cook what we like to eat too. In terms of service, our staff are encouraged to create an environment that they would feel comfortable in, which probably makes it easier to pull off, as there is no pretention. *They* set the tone.

Tastes change gradually, and whether we're dictating some of these changes, or we're following trends, as long as we're always moving we feel that our staff and customers will continue to be interested. I genuinely believe that part of the reason we are busy is that people can feel that we're enthusiastic (OK, 'passionate') about what we do. I work full time on the premises, we have low staff turnover and we're situated in a small town within minutes from Belfast by car, so through serving a lot of the same customers regularly over time, good relationships are built.

We have definitely based a lot of our menu decisions on feedback from customers – what they'd like us to do, what they really didn't like us doing and what they'd like us to *keep* doing. Unfortunately, despite the desire to only take the praise, you have to listen to it all, whether you initially/ultimately agree with it or not.

Our 'famous' cinnamon scones recently went through a torrid time when we bought a new oven, as we had been so used to cooking them with our previous equipment. We got an incredible amount of criticism that they were too dry, the recipe was different and they weren't as good as they used to be. Whilst we were rightly concerned, the geeky part of us loved the fact that people had such a vested interest in our (their) product. We played around with the oven, trying this or that, here and there, all the while keeping our customers posted and seeking their feedback until we were confident we'd got it right. In some ways, through this potentially difficult couple of months we formed a stronger relationship with certain customers. Having said that, we probably did lose a few who thought we had simply lost our touch. But the point still stands!

Another obvious but difficult thing to get right is staff. You know when you've got a good team, just as you know when you've got a bad team. You're not going to keep a strong group together forever, and we've learnt (the hard way) that you shouldn't *keep* the weak ones together either. Our customers over the years have also been able to identify the standard of any given group of employees. Whether it's a compliment or criticism, they've told us, told their friends and written about it online. So we make sure we select staff carefully, check references and are not afraid to make a tricky decision within a probationary period if needs be. It sounds like, and *is*, an unpleasant and essentially ruthless thing to do, but if you don't, you might be stuck with somebody who can affect the reputation of your business for quite a while. I should point out that we have a FANTASTIC team at the minute!

JOHNNY – SIDE STORY

I've worked with William Farmer (and previously his mother Sue) for many years. During that time the ownership of the business has shifted and now William is the sole owner.

This is often a difficult thing to do. The business had been very successful in its previous guise but much of that didn't completely fit into William's vision of the business he wanted to own and run. His gentle and highly effective changes have created a business that he can now be passionate about without losing an ounce of the charm that Sue created over the years.

William Farmer's one-sentence takeaway

Get close and really listen to your regular customers, but always contain this within the passion and the vision for what you want to do and what will make you enthusiastic about getting out of bed each morning.

CONCLUSIONS

Hugh and I have been discussing this project for many years, but neither of us expected to receive such great insight from so many great people. Ultimately, we ended up with far more information and responses than can be contained within this book, so please make sure you go to www.wakeupandsellbook. com to get access to the extended interviews, the larger piece of research that was also undertaken and the webinars we produced to help you apply this knowledge to your business.

In terms of the proof or discrediting of our formula, it almost seems churlish to say that the comments we got very closely mirror the formula that we developed. To a large extent that's really not surprising. Our formula isn't rocket science, by any means – it's simply a distillation of many years working in and with an increasingly large and global base of great coffee shops and cafés.

Out of the interviews, and wider research, there are ten key recurring themes that I think are worth developing.

1. Passion – Arguably the most nebulous part of the formula, this is a recurring theme in a huge number of the responses. There is absolutely no doubt in my mind that the really successful operators, in any area of catering and hospitality, are driven by a passionate desire to produce great food and drink. These people, in many cases, drive their wives, husbands, friends and children mad with this passion.

But what also comes through is a strong sense of joy that accompanies this passion. An acceptance that passion for great food or coffee, even when it tips into obsession, isn't necessarily a bad thing. It can and should be a lot of fun.

2. Hospitality – This was a frequent theme and one that I've been attempting to bang on about in the past. What shone through, though, was that it has to be instinctive. It cannot be overly manufactured or scripted. You need to want to welcome people into your business and serve them. Operators like Philip Ash and Peter Dore-Smith have this at an instinctive level, but for others it must be part of a process – both for the owner or manager themselves and for the staff.

Within the wider research, which included a selection of much less successful coffee shops and cafés, there are some respondents who are clearly frustrated by customer behaviour and their inability to bend them to their will. Frustration at customer behaviour is a one-way ticket to the bankruptcy court.

You'll also notice that a large majority of the interviewees mention the importance of the recruitment process in getting friendly people – the technical skills can always be taught; smiling with ease and a natural desire to want to make customers happy cannot.

3. Bring staff along for the journey – If I'm honest this is never something I have managed as well as some of these guys. Peter Dore-smith and Carl Sara (an Australian and a New

Zealander . . . perhaps there's a lesson there) are both incredibly open about developing people within their business and the industry for the good of all.

James Shapland did something similar in Coffee #1 – he built a team around him with a crystal clear vision of an outcome (in his case a sale), but made very sure that he trained and developed them along the way and ensured they were financially rewarded when that sale happened.

4. Treat it like a business – I can't avoid saying it. But really if there was one message that I wanted to get across that came out of these interviews, it was this. And don't forget, not one single interviewee was pushed or cajoled into specific answers by Hugh or myself. We simply wanted to get the honest feedback. Almost without exception the owners of these highly successful businesses emphasise the need to treat your coffee shop as a business and have a rigorous grasp of the finances.

5. The wider coffee community – There's no doubt that there is a wonderful and supportive worldwide coffee community. Perhaps Stephen Leighton put it best when he described how he has multiple sofas around the world to sleep on!

This is rare for a business community and it's a great thing. Coffee shop owners, especially the passionate and good ones, are bound together by some sort of invisible brotherhood. You can see it at the multiple worldwide meet-ups that occur which, in many cases, really don't fall into the same category as normal trade shows for other industries.

If you're not tapping into this you're probably making your job a little more lonely and harder work than it needs to be.

6. Dedication and patience – It's quite clear that success doesn't happen overnight. Pascal Wrenn's story illustrates this in graphic detail and shows how important it is to keep going when times are tough.

David Schomer doesn't mention it in his piece, but it takes a barista on average eighteen months before he is allowed to serve at the counter in one of his stores. That's patience.

So don't rush it. Take the time to build something really great and with strong foundations.

7. Hard graft – This is another repeated theme. There will be late nights, early mornings, phone calls on your day off and broken windows at 3 a.m. Your drains will block and you might even find a tramp insisting on sleeping in your toilets – or, and its not a story for this book (because it's so revolting) perhaps doing something else, rather publicly . . .

Much of this, but not all, can be eased with great operational systems, but you have to accept that this is an intensive business that almost starts from a blank sheet every day – that's either a good thing or a bad thing depending upon your view of hospitality and your passion for the food and drink you serve.

8. Build an asset – This wasn't talked about as much as I'd have liked. Peter Dore-Smith talked about it and one of my business colleagues, John Davy (who has built and sold many businesses, including the Jongleurs chain of comedy clubs, for many millions), extensively touched on it in his interview. John's interview didn't make the final cut primarily because we chose to keep the emphasis on coffee shops and cafés, but you can find the full process that he and I have worked on to build a business for sale in the accompanying material.

It's a critical part of the jigsaw. As you can tell from point seven, this isn't going to be easy and your retirement will hopefully be long and filled with travel to meet all your new-found coffee friends dotted around the world.

For goodness' sake make sure you have a business that you can sell and enjoy this retirement.

9. Tread lightly and with great focus on the fine line between customer feedback and compromise – Throughout the interviews you'll see numerous mentions of how important it is to listen to your customers and yet you'll also find a lot of advice on how you must stay true to your vision. Paradoxically both views are correct. It's up to you to make the judgement call between what your customers are demanding and what you want to serve.

As ever though, the till doesn't lie. Going right back to the confirmation bias mentioned at the beginning – if your till readings are falling then you need to change.

The whole area of customer feedback is beyond the scope of this book, but the simplest analogy I use is one that I learned from Gordon Ramsay. I was privileged to be able to work alongside him as the 'coffee shop expert' for one of his TV programmes as he trained up a group of prisoners to create products for sale to the retail market.

There is a lot to learn from him and his attention to detail and response to feedback. The product he had created with the prisoners was too sweet. It might have worked as a dessert in a restaurant, but to accompany a sweetened latte in a large chain (which was the market he was aiming for) the balance was off.

It was with a certain trepidation that I explained to him, on camera, that his product wasn't right – he took the advice very well and told me he would change it on my advice. Since the production company was partly owned by him, I doubted this wouldn't make the final edit. When it did, and he responded off camera in a very positive way about my feedback, I was very surprised.

Afterwards, I learnt that at the weekly meetings for his restaurants they take all the letters and feedback forms from the previous week and put them into two piles. Pile one is the praise pile. These are discarded and not read by Ramsay. Instead he goes through, with the relevant staff, every complaint and makes sure that the mistake doesn't happen again and the issue is fixed.

That's how you need to deal with feedback. Remove your ego and confirmation bias and make sure that you fix any issues and, so long as they are reasonable and within your vision, make changes to keep the customer happy. Sé Gorman touched on this within his piece, too.

I would recommend re-reading Stephen Leighton's story of his first coffee shop to see how dumbing down and listening to feedback the wrong way can destroy your business.

10. Responsibility – As Jack Groot says, 'The buck stops with you'. If I had to pick one thing and one thing alone, taking 100 per cent responsibility for your business would be the one. Hugh, totally independently of me, also lists this. And, if you read between the lines of practically every interviewee you'll find similar stories of taking total responsibility.

CHANGES TO THE GREAT FORMULA

At the beginning of this project we were looking to test this formula – attempting to see if it really matched up with the experience of the very best operators out there. Did our seven steps, despite undergoing extensive testing in our own businesses and with clients, genuinely correspond with what great coffee shop and café owners had discovered themselves?

By and large the answer is yes. Amongst the really successful operators there wasn't anything that strongly conflicted with what Hugh and I teach, and in many cases there was an almost carbon copy of lessons being taught.

But the whole process made me think much deeply about the business and what marks out the great ones. It made me think a lot about the character of the successful guys versus those who still struggle, and those who dart in, searching for the 'quick buck', and leave, tail between their legs, blaming the big chains for ruining everything.

James Shapland's story about opening on either side of Starbucks shows, more graphically that any other I've heard in the UK, that a great independent can comfortably beat the big chains at their game. In another site of his we measured sales 40 per cent up on a consistent basis against a different one of the big three – despite its location in a better site four doors down a busy high street.

So it can be done. And it is being done, very competently, by the vast majority of respondents in this book. This isn't a Starbucks/Costa/Nero bashing point – I actually think they bring huge value to the average battered and bruised high street. They create vibrancy, buzz and footfall for other beleaguered retailers to feed from.

The point really is that you can and should be able to compete with the big chains – it may not be easy but the lessons in this book, coupled with our own advice as well as that of others who have 'been there and done it', shows that a road map for success can be followed. But it does take a certain type of person to do that and those people need to become leaders – they need to make sure they can take their vision and passion and consistently instil that in staff and customers.

The second issue is the concept of exit strategy. The flaw of this book, in terms of testing the formula, is that in most cases we're dealing with historical information, coupled with advice for what to do now, and being taught by people who are still in business. That leaves a gap for what happens at the end.

Our work with coffee shop owners and hospitality businesses in general shows that in many cases the issue of how to exit with a decent return on your time and money is strongly overlooked. This industry, filled as it is with so many passionate people, tends to discourage conversations about how you get out and actually leave with some money! So that's a critical part of the formula that needs to be addressed.

With that said, there are now two additions to our Great Formula, highlighted in the list below. And we're extremely grateful to all concerned for helping us shift in this direction.

1. Passion – As mentioned in the conclusion in my ten takeaways, this is as important as ever. Great food and great drinks will always require passionate people, at all levels.

2. Product/Taste – All the greats go to seemingly crazy extremes to ensure that what is served is of as high a quality as possible. Out of twenty-two interviews there isn't one single story about how 'cutting corners' or using cheaper ingredients is a reasonable strategy to develop profits.

To see real passion for taste in evidence make sure you read Hugo Hercod's submission again, and for essential ongoing reading bookmark Peter Dore-Smith's Kaffeine blog.

3. Positioning – Both the interviewees and our wider research shows that it's vital to make sure you're correctly positioned for the right audience. David Schomer has arguably the best story on this, but remember this is about much more than just location.

4. Leadership – A new entry (in old-school top 40 terms). What we've discovered is that without solid leadership this whole formula falls apart. The creation of a great business in this industry requires what can only be described as a bit of 'magic'. Our extensive research between great coffee shops and poor ones via video, hundreds of hours of in-person observation, and meticulous poring over figures shows that 'the one thing' that makes the biggest difference between a great store and bad one (within the same chain) is great leadership from managers.

Jo Hamilton-Welsman from Coffee #1 has demonstrated, time and time again, that a good manager can drive record-breaking sales in underperforming stores.

But great managers need great leadership from the owners. Great managers generally have no interest in working for people who aren't great leaders or who don't have a strong and passionate vision for the business and the future. So any success in this business requires that the owner must step up to the leadership plate and be constantly leading, developing and working with the staff at all levels to ensure they are fully 'bought in'.

There simply isn't enough profit in coffee shops and cafés to entice your employees by money alone. So your staff, and especially the really great ones, are never in it just for the money – you need to lead them and bring them along with a vision of something they can be really proud of.

In the last ten years we've held countless one-day seminars on various aspects of the business such as marketing, finances and recruitment, but the only one that has to be a two-day course is leadership. And even that should really be a three-day course but it's hard to persuade people to take three days off work. Leadership is so important though. It's the intangible that makes the biggest difference of all and you can see how, without exception, the natural tone of the leader comes through in each interview.

5. People – If there was one single aspect of the formula that was most emphasised it was this. The recruitment of great people, who care about the customer and service, is clearly more important than the technical skills.

Stephen Hurst goes so far as to state: 'It's still all about the people' twice in his list – and that's from someone at the very core of coffee supply.

The simplest way to think about it is in a quadrant with four distinct aspects that you must be constantly working on, as follows:

Quadrant One – Recruitment. Making sure you have great people who really care about the customer experience . . . and never just about a great coffee or brownie. And the golden rule of recruitment: create a business that people want to work for.

Quadrant Two – Induction. You absolutely must have solid induction training programmes in place to help people integrate into your business – even if you are just one site. Check out the stories of David Schomer and Jo from Coffee #1 to see a little more of this.

Quadrant Three – Retention/development. You've got to hold on to and develop these people. You've got to make them want to stay, even if they can make more money elsewhere. But you also have to accept that in this industry staff are always transient to some degree. You're rarely going to have people who stay with you for more than five or ten years. So build them up, develop them and, as in the case of Peter Dore-Smith, help them out if they want to go and open their own store. Remember this industry involves a community like no other – embrace, rather than reject, that.

Quadrant Four – Customer behaviour. You've got to be become a mix of investigative journalist, psychiatrist, psychologist and anthropologist. You, and your staff, must be constantly curious and attempting to work out what the customer is thinking, wanting and which way they're going to jump. Constantly elicit feedback and never stop 'wearing customer shoes'.

If you can continually work on those four you'll make life a lot easier for yourself. Unfortunately, the 'people' aspect doesn't end there. You'll need to be very aware of how to deal with partners, lenders, suppliers, landlords, government bodies and even competitors. Whatever way you look at it, you need to be a people person to thrive in this industry.

6. Systems/Processes. In the last few years we've tended to shift from systems thinking towards talking about processes. It's semantics really, but can often be seen by managers and owners as a more acceptable term to help them manage the business.

But, whatever you call it, you must have processes in place to manage the business properly. There is often a sense amongst new starts that this isn't important because 'they're going to be there anyway', especially if there is no desire to create a larger chain, but this is a perfect recipe for exhaustion, frustration, and ultimately failure if you fall ill and cannot be in the business for a month or so.

The value of systems and processes for, as much as is possible, everything in your business cannot be overestimated. Check out Pascal Wrenn's story to see how important they were to the growth and development of his business.

7. Marketing. This will always remain on the list, but it is, to use a footballing analogy (and I know absolutely nothing about football), a game of two halves. In many cases, as long as you have a good location, there is very little you need to do from an external marketing (i.e. increasing footfall with new customers) perspective. A great coffee shop, genuinely and consistently serving great food and beverages, will not struggle to be busy. If you have a great location and you're not busy, then I'm afraid there's something wrong with your core business and not doing enough marketing to get people through the door won't make a blind bit of difference.

This is a difficult truth for many to understand and accept. But marketing is a complex mix that extends way beyond getting new customers through the door. Coffee #1 grew with almost no marketing to drive new customers through the door in any way. Kaffeine does almost no marketing apart from Twitter and regular updates on the blog.

With that in mind we split our marketing advice into four, very distinct, categories or zones:

Zone One – everything that you do to get a new customer to the front door. This includes tools such as sampling, advertising, signage, direct marketing, joint ventures and public relations. All of this will be necessary if you have a site in a location that isn't immediately obvious – see Devinder Dhallu's take on this for a great example of what needs to be done.

Zone Two – everything that happens between the front door and the till. In other words, everything that you do to ensure that customer spend is as high as possible. Your variables here are almost infinite. To begin with you must be aware of all the senses experienced by the customer – sight, sound, taste, touch and smell. Working through each of those will help you create an atmosphere that makes the customer feel welcome and trust that you're going to serve them well.

That's the absolute tip of the iceberg, though – you need a surgeon's attention to detail with things like your menu design and wording, merchandising units (our ten golden rules for this are included in the supporting material), general layout of counters and staff positioning, uniforms and greetings.

Zone Three – the epicentre. This is, for a counter-service operation, everything that happens between the handing over of money at the till and the customer taking their first sip of coffee or bite of sandwich. It's a little zone or process that is often ignored by owners but which can make or break the overall experience of the customer – often at an unconscious level.

Zone Four – everything you do to make sure the customer returns. Once you've gone to the effort of having the customer visit you, the big issue is ensuring that they return – and return often. One master of this is Philip Ash – remembering names, drinks, holidays, sports and any other information he can in an effort to create a community centre as much as a coffee shop. Again, it's worth noting that Philip has done zero external marketing (zone one) for any of his shops.

It's in zone four, whether you like it or not, that social media is so important. Twitter, Facebook, Instagram and the myriad other channels allow you to reach out to and remind customers of your presence whilst they're sitting at their desks or lying flicking through a tablet on the sofa at home. This is how you reinforce the community aspect, how you demonstrate the effort you put into taste and show that you're a business with a passionate soul.

8. Money/Finances. This was consistently emphasised by a large majority of the respondents and interviewees. Carl Sara talks about the importance of 'not running a coffee shop but a business that is a coffee shop'. It's an important distinction.

David Schomer, arguably one of the most obsessive coffee specialists the industry has ever seen, mentions, more than once, the importance of very strict financial controls and processes. Hugo Hercod talks about the importance of loving the financial side of the business and how this knowledge has saved his bacon on more than one occasion.

It's a non-negotiable part of the business – even if you don't understand the numbers properly yourself make sure you have somebody (like Geneva Sullivan in David Schomer's case) who can be on top of this at all times for you.

9. Exit. Another new entry. Really, this formula for coffee shop success should have always had this in place. At school, during English class, we were all taught that a story needs a 'Beginning, a middle and an end'. Our formula simply takes you to the middle of the story.

But the end is critical. You must, as Peter Dore-Smith puts it, be prepared to think of your business as a product in itself. There must be an end in mind. You might not be quite as focused as James Shapland was for his outcome, but it absolutely must be there in the back of your mind somewhere.

And it needs to be there right at the start. We consistently advise owners who have made fundamental mistakes, in an effort to get the business open quickly, which means that they are working very hard to create a business that ultimately has no worth. The biggest mistakes are made with landlords and lease terms, but there are many other considerations you should have in mind, too.

A brutal reality of single-site coffee shops is that the value of the business is likely to be three times your net profit – at best. Starbucks, at the time of writing, is valued at approximately twenty times its yearly profit. Quite a difference.

This difference in income multiples is something that you can work on and adjust though, and it is something you should be aware of as you take any major steps forward with your business. But there are multiple other factors to be aware of too, such as location, potential buyers, local competitors and economic cycles. It's beyond the remit of this book to go into these in great depth, but we have extensive interviews and extra information on this in the bonus information available at www.wakeupandsellbook.com.

So that's it – a revised formula for success based on nearly 1000 interviews and insight from twenty-two of the best in the world. Of course, as is now abundantly clear, actually applying this formula to your business is not the work of a weekend . . .